WOMEN OF LIGHT

WOMEN OF LIGHT

BY WALTER RUSSELL BOWIE

Harper & Row · Publishers · New York · Evanston · London

1228

LIBRARY OF CONGRESS CATALOG CARD NUMBER: 63-20285

E-Q

To
JEAN
In whose soul and in whose eyes
the eternal Light was shining

Acknowledgements

THE AUTHOR IS GRATEFUL TO LISA MCGAW FOR EXPERT EDITORIAL ASSISTANCE.

Grateful acknowledgement is made to the following for permission to reprint material from the works indicated:

CURTIS BROWN, LTD.: *Saint Joan of Arc* by V. Sackville-West (published by Doubleday, Doran & Company), copyright 1931 by Curtis Brown, Ltd. (permission also from Michael Joseph, Ltd.)

THE EPWORTH PRESS: *The Journal of the Rev. John Wesley* edited by Nehemiah Curnock, copyright 1909 by The Epworth Press.

HARPER & ROW, PUBLISHERS, INCORPORATED: *This Is My Story* by Eleanor Roosevelt, copyright 1937 by Anna Eleanor Roosevelt (permission also from Laurence Pollinger, Ltd.); *The Autobiography of Eleanor Roosevelt*, copyright © 1961 by Anna Eleanor Roosevelt (permission also from The Hutchinson Publishing Group).

HODDER AND STOUGHTON, LTD.: *The World I Live In* by Helen Keller, copyright 1908 by Hodder and Stoughton, Ltd.

HOLT, RINEHART AND WINSTON, INC.: *Chicago Poems* by Carl Sandburg, copyright 1916, 1944 by Holt, Rinehart and Winston, Inc.

MACMILLAN & CO., LTD.: *The Life of Florence Nightingale* by Edward Cook, copyright 1913 by Macmillan & Co., Ltd.

THE MACMILLAN COMPANY: *Jane Addams of Hull House* by Margaret Tims, copyright © 1961 by The Macmillan Company; *Twenty Years at Hull House* by Jane Addams, copyright 1910 by The Macmillan Company.

MCGRAW HILL BOOK COMPANY: *Florence Nightingale* by Cecil Woodham-Smith, copyright 1951 by McGraw Hill Book Company.

G. P. PUTNAM'S SONS: *Mrs. R., The Life of Eleanor Roosevelt* by Alfred Steinberg, copyright 1958 by G. P. Putnam's Sons.

THE UNIVERSITY OF NORTH CAROLINA PRESS: *The Jeanes Teacher in the United States* by Lance G. E. Jones, copyright 1937 by The University of North Carolina Press.

VANGUARD PRESS, INC.: *Mary McLeod Bethune* by Catherine Owens Peare, copyright 1951 by Vanguard Press, Inc.

JANET WHITNEY: *Elizabeth Fry, Quaker Heroine* by Janet Whitney, copyright 1936 by Janet Whitney.

THOMAS YOSELOFF, INC.: *A Whisper of Eternity* by A. A. Hoehling, copyright 1957 by Thomas Yoseloff, Inc.

Contents

Contents

Foreword

This book is a companion to the previously published *Men of Fire*, which had to do with some of the great masculine figures in history from biblical times down to the present day. In those men there was the driving force which fire at first suggests. But the fire in human souls can have many aspects. It can be a flame which has power—and also peril—in it; it can also be warm and comforting and protective; and it can shine like a lamp to penetrate the shadows and make a safer progress into the unknown. It is in this gentler way that the flame which burns in the souls of women may be most manifest. That is why this book is entitled *Women of Light*.

For the kind of influence, then, which women exemplify, and which the pages that follow would portray, let one picture be the illustration. It comes from a man's remembrance of what one woman, his mother, had meant to him.

Father Andrew, as he was called when he became a member of the small monastic Society of Divine Compassion, was Henry Ernest Hardy, a priest of the Church of England. His father commanded a regiment of native troops of the British army in India in the middle of the nineteenth century, when India was a dominion of the British crown. The admiration which his men had for him was such that he held their loyalty through the terrible days of the Indian mutiny. After the mutiny, he was in one part of India and his wife in another. She set out to join him, by a long journey through the jungle, accompanied only by a few Indian servants. One night in a hut alongside the jungle trail she was sitting with a book in her hands, reading by the light of a lamp. In the corner of the hut, wrapped up and asleep, was her baby, the future Father Andrew. Suddenly she was aware of something near her, and there on the floor of the hut was the crouched body of a huge panther, its head pointing toward the baby. Rising instantly, she seized the lamp and thrust it into the great beast's face. The panther drew back, and leaped snarling through the wide window space and disappeared into the jungle, carrying with him a kid that had been tethered outside the hut.

Long afterward Father Andrew, remembering what he had been told of the events that night by the jungle trail, wrote this tribute to his mother:

> It has always seemed to me that that incident is a parable of what my mother has been to me: a gracious presence, beautiful, courageous, and compact of love, ready at any time to put herself between me and danger, and with the light that she herself possessed to drive back into the night any treacherous thing that might draw near to harm me.[1]

"The light that she herself possessed." Through those words a great vista of thought and imagination opens. Most history has been written by men and about men. Their roles have been more dramatic and therefore more conspicuous, and certainly the story of the human race has been ennobled by those who in the arena of militant achievement have been the *Men of Fire*. However, there is a light which is not the sudden blaze of torches, but the quiet shining of a lamp. This is what women at their best have been and are. They have possessed within themselves the quality of spirit from which the great ideals of courage and of sacrifice have been kindled in our human race. This book, therefore, has to do with some of the women who

---

[1] Kathleen E. Burne (ed.), *The Life and Letters of Father Andrew* (London: A. R. Mowbray, 1948), p. 10.

have been great; not in the self-assertiveness which may be the quickest way to personal fame, but in the self-forgetfulness which stands between some other life and danger, and with the inner light which womanhood possesses can "drive back into the night any treacherous thing that might draw near to harm."

WOMEN OF LIGHT

❦ I ❧

Great Women of the Bible

In the early periods of human evolution the woman was held in scant respect. Brute strength was what counted then. It was through the spirit of Jesus that there came a new recognition of the strength that might be in gentleness. In the time covered by the Old Testament and on into the period of the New Testament, women are still in the background. But one can begin to see their faces, and on their faces there is light.

Sometimes a woman comes into fleeting view through only a single reference. In the Book of Genesis (35:8) it is recorded that Deborah, the nurse of Rebekah, died and was buried under the oak of weeping. Nothing else is said of her, but imagination kindles at what those words imply. Here was one who had no prominence, and in whose life was no single event significant enough to be recorded. Yet as Rebekah's nurse she had been part of a family's life, woven into the pattern of its everyday existence, her faithfulness a familiar thing, taken perhaps for granted and not much noticed—until she died, and then those whom she had loved and served knew all at once the void that she had left, and buried her "under the oak of weeping." From the far-off centuries the words come down, but the reality which lies back of them reappears in every generation. Who can number the men and women who have looked back in gratitude to the nurse they knew when they were little children? Robert Louis Stevenson dedicated *A Child's Garden of Verses* to "Alison Cunningham, from Her Boy,"

> For the long nights you lay awake
> And watched for my unworthy sake.

And his dedication ended with his prayer that every child may find as dear a nurse at need, and hear

> as kind a voice
> As made my childish days rejoice.

In the Book of Exodus there is another swift allusion which awakened interest would follow further if it could. A Pharaoh in Egypt has grown apprehensive concerning the possible subversive danger that the Hebrew slaves in his land may represent, and he has decreed that all boy children should be slain. A baby born to a Hebrew mother is hidden by her among the reeds by the Nile River. If he is found by Pharaoh's officers, that will be his end. But who finds him? The daughter of Pharaoh, coming with her maids to bathe. She sees a basket that had been woven out of bulrushes, and curious as to what it might be she sends one of the maids to fetch it. "When she opened it, she saw the child; and lo, the babe was crying" (Exod. 2:6). She saw too that this was one of the Hebrew children. To protect him might be perilous. Nevertheless, "she took pity on him." And by her pity, according to the immortal story which has come down in the Book of Exodus, the whole drama of history would be affected. For the child she took from the river, and who was handed back for a while to his own mother to be suckled, was taken presently by the princess to Pharaoh's palace to be brought up as though he were her son. This child, grown into a man, was Moses: Moses, who was to leave behind him all that he might have had in Egypt, and become the leader to set the Hebrew people free.

By the banks of the Nile that day when she found the baby, the daughter of Pharaoh could not have known or imagined the destinies that were at stake, but those destinies depended in that moment on the emotions in her heart. To Pharaoh's officers this child would have been only a pawn in the policies of Egypt, to be sacrificed without compunction. But what she saw was the helplessness to which her instinctive womanhood responded. Her instant pity was stronger than any cautious thought she might have had as to what was safe and prudent, and so she acted as she did. In the swift and fragmentary narrative, nothing more is told of her: nothing of how she managed to be allowed to adopt this child, nothing of the way she may have mothered him. But whatever in the Book of Exodus account may be historic fact and what portion a beautiful tradition, the story as it is reflects a recognition of that which has been true since human life existed. It is the woman who cherishes the weakness which, through her, may grow into strength. All that a man in his career goes on to accomplish may trace back, as did the career of Moses, to the protectiveness which in some critical moment a woman gave.

One of the loveliest books of the Old Testament—also one of the shortest, which writings about women were likely to be—is the Book of Ruth. Its keynote is struck in its opening chapter. A man of Israel and his two sons had been driven by famine into Moab, which was enemy country. The sons married; then both of them, and also the father, died; and Naomi, their mother, was left with the girls they had married, Orpah and Ruth. Naomi will go back now to her own land of Israel. Both of her daughters-in-law are sad at the thought of separation; yet, sad as the separation is, going out of Moab seems to Orpah something that would be worse. She weeps, and kisses her mother-in-law—but then she says goodbye. Ruth is different. For good or ill, she clings to Naomi. "Entreat me not to leave you or to return from following you," she said. "Where you go I will go, and where you lodge, I will lodge; your people shall be my people, and your God my God; where you die I will die, and there will I be buried. May the Lord do so to me and more also if even death parts me from you" (Ruth 1:16-17).

Ruth goes with Naomi into Israel, leaving her own land behind. The significance of the book is in the fact that between Moab and Israel there had been old and bitter hatred; but the tie which Ruth had with the woman who had become to her as a mother was precious enough to be worth all that it could cost. So she will come into a new life and an unfamiliar land and make them her own, notwithstanding what must have been the lonely hours of wistfulness

> . . . when, sick for home,
> she stood in tears amid the alien corn.[1]

The details of the picture change, but in its central fact it does not disappear. The loyalty of Ruth is the loyalty that women have shown so often that it is hardly counted as remarkable. Yet it is the inmost strength of those relationships which keep the precious values of our human life. Men can be loyal too; but it is the woman who usually embodies the loyalty that costs most; of daughter to mother, of wife to the husband whose name she has taken and whose lot she completely shares, of mother to the child whom she will love and believe in even if all the world has turned against him.

In the Gospel according to Luke there is the account of a woman who appears in a startling way. Jesus had been invited to the house of a Pharisee named Simon. In Palestine at the time the first act of courteous hospitality was to have the dusty sandals of the guest removed and his feet bathed, but this had been neglected. In contrast to the indifference of the Pharisee there came now an act of prodigal devotion. "A woman of the city, who was a sinner," when she learned that Jesus was in Simon's house, made her uninvited entrance and fell on her knees at Jesus' feet. Weeping, she wiped his feet with her loosened hair, and anointed them from an alabaster box of precious ointment. Simon was outraged. What was it but defilement to his house that this despised woman should brazenly come across its threshold? And as for Jesus—the Pharisee muttered, "If this man were a prophet, he would have known who and what sort of woman this is who is touching him, for she is a sinner" (Luke 7:36-39).

But Jesus looked deeper. To him she was not "this sort of woman"; not someone to be known by a general label, but a particular soul in need. He turned to the Pharisee. "Simon," he said, "I have something to say to you. . . . Do you see this woman? I entered your house, you gave me no water for my feet, but she has wet my feet with her tears and wiped them with her hair. You gave me no kiss, but from the time I came in she has not ceased to kiss my feet. You did not anoint my head with oil, but she has anointed my feet with ointment. Therefore, I tell you, her sins, which are many, are forgiven, for she loved much" (Luke 7:40, 44-47).

Where she may have seen Jesus before, and what she may have heard him say, we do not know; but whatever it may have been, it was enough to work a transformation. For the first time she saw in Jesus what a life could be: in purity, in strength, in tenderness; and all her heart turned toward it with a sobbing thankfulness, as a lost child in a dark wood turns toward a sudden light that shows the way home. She could love the highest when she saw it, and in that love was the power that could loose her from her sins.

The Gospel does not give the name of this woman who knelt at Jesus' feet. It has sometimes been conjectured that she may have been Mary Magdalene, and if so, there is added knowledge as to the witness that her life would bear. Out of her, as this same Gospel according to Luke says, "had gone seven devils." Kahlil Gibran, in *Jesus, The Son Of Man*, gives as from Mary's lips the description of what had happened to her soul when she first encountered Jesus.

> It was in the month of June when I saw Him for the first time. . . .
> . . . I was dead. I was a woman who had divorced her soul. I was living apart from this self which you now see. I belonged to all men, and to none. . . .
> Then He looked at me, and the noontide of His eyes was upon me, and He said, . . . "Other men see a beauty

in you that shall fade away sooner than their own
years. But I see in you a beauty that shall not fade
away, and in the autumn of your days that beauty
shall not be afraid to gaze at itself in the mirror, and it
shall not be offended.

I alone love the unseen in you." . . .

And then He walked away.

But no other man ever walked the way He walked.
Was it a breath born in my garden that moved to the
east? Or was it a storm that would shake all things to
their foundations?

I know not; but on that day the sunset of His eyes
slew the dragon in me, and I became a woman. . . .[2]

This same Mary Magdalene would be one of those who henceforth clung to him with unbounded loyalty. She would stand
with Jesus' mother at the foot of the cross, and she would be
one of the first to see the risen Christ on Easter day. So she has
become an exemplar of that which may be in all Christian souls,
but may be most luminous in women: a response to the grace of
God as seen in Jesus so sensitive that by it their own lives and
the lives of all they touch will be refined.

In the New Testament there is a reference which brings a
flash of swift suggestion like that in the Old Testament reference
to Deborah. At the end of the letter to the Romans comes a long
list of greetings which the apostle Paul was sending to some who
were especially dear to him. The list begins, "Greet Prisca and
Aquila, my fellow workers in Christ Jesus." Then presently
comes this: "Greet Rufus, eminent in the Lord, also his mother
and mine" (16:3, 13).

That is all; but it is like the momentary opening of a door
through which one gets an instant glimpse within the house to
which it opens, as one passes by. Evidently there had been a
time when Paul had been welcomed in the house of Rufus—
whoever Rufus may have been. And it was not only Rufus

whom he remembered gratefully. There was Rufus' mother who had taken him into her solicitude, so that she seemed his mother too. Her name is not written down, for the simple reason that everybody who would read Paul's letter knew it; and it is not necessary for us to know her name in order for her figure to come alive again in our imagination. We do not always think of the apostle Paul just as a human being. He seems to stride so ahead of us and above us in his achievements that we tend to regard him as in every way remote: caught up in his tremendous purposes, tireless in endurance, his thought related to vast theological horizons beyond the ken of ordinary people. What need did he have to sit down before the hearth-fire of the little intimate affections? Yet Paul must often have needed exactly that, and the loneliness in him must have cried out for it. No casual recollection only, but an enduring gratitude throbs in the message he sends "to Rufus, also his mother and mine."

It would seem that there would be a great deal to be read and clearly known in the New Testament record about the woman who above all others has been most reverenced: Mary, the mother of Jesus. But that is not the fact. What is told of her is fragmentary, and the fragments do not always fit together into the expected picture. Theologians have written endlessly about her, but much that was written has been conjecture, shaped by the assumptions which were already in the particular writer's mind.

In the introductory chapters of Matthew and Luke there are the beautiful stories current in the early church of the coming of the Archangel Gabriel to the Maid of Nazareth and his message that the Savior should be born of her. Luke tells also of how, when Jesus was twelve years old, his mother and Joseph took him to Jerusalem for the Passover, and of what happened there; and that Mary "kept all these things in her heart" (Luke 2:51). But after Jesus began his public ministry, the name of Mary is in the record hardly at all. It is said that she was in Jerusalem at the crucifixion; and with the disciples in the Upper

Room at Pentecost. But in between she appears only once or twice, and then in a way that sounds strangely out of tune with the cult of superhuman greatness which has been built about her. It would seem that she was bewildered and troubled about this great Son of hers, who to the neighbors was so inexplicable. There was a day when some of his friends "went out to seize him, for they said, 'He is beside himself'" (Mark 3:21). It may have been with anxious desire to get him home that Mary went to seek him on a day after that. In the midst of the crowd that flocked about him, Jesus was told, "Your mother and your brothers are standing outside, desiring to see you." But he said to them, "My mother and my brothers are those who hear the word of God and do it" (Luke 8:20-21).

Some years ago there was written and enacted a drama called *Family Portrait*,[3] which had to do with the family in Nazareth. Jesus himself never directly appeared, either in figure or in voice, but the excitement of what he was, and of what he was doing, throbbed through it like a chord of underlying music. The portrayal there of Mary was always reverent, and at the same time so searching in its simplicity that one's thought instinctively responded, "This is how she really was." For the Mary one saw and heard had in her all the pathos of her humanness as well as the wonder that glowed in her from the divineness of her Son.

It is this human motherhood of Mary, wistful, brooding, and often troubled, that is most manifest in the record of the Gospels. Nothing that Mary said or did during the period of Jesus' ministry had any supernatural aspect. Nor was there need of anything supernatural in her in order that her womanhood should be reckoned as forever beautiful. She was not appointed to redeem the world; her sufficient glory was that among all the women of the earth it was she who was appointed to bear and nurture the one who would be the Redeemer. "The Word became flesh and dwelt among us" (John 1:14). Jesus came not as some full-grown embodiment of heavenly power, but as a baby laid in a woman's arms. And those arms were Mary's. Who can measure therefore all that she gave him in the years when the little boy looked up into her face; when she told him the stories written in the Scriptures, sang to him the psalms, taught him his people's agelong prayers for the Redeemer who would come? No wonder it would be true, as in the prophetic words of her Magnificat, that "henceforth all generations will call me blessed" (Luke 1:48).

But the extraordinary fact is that Mary of Nazareth, with all her lovely humanness, has been translated into a divine figure far removed from the reality of the Gospels. She has been made the center of an adoration which in a great part of Christendom almost eclipses recognition of the redemption that comes through Christ. In the Dark Ages and in the medieval centuries, the thought of the church had fallen back to a warped idea of God in which the redeeming beauty of what Jesus had revealed was lost. Before Christ, men chiefly thought of God as the august Power to be feared, relentless in judgment, implacable to human weaknesses and sins. But Jesus had brought to human hearts the message of God's infinite compassion and his outreaching love: a love of God that is like the shepherd going out to find the one lost sheep, or the father waiting unweariedly for the prodigal son to come home. The instinctive yearning of men who felt their guilt and helplessness responded to that gospel; and always there is a soul-hunger for which no gospel less than that can be the adequate good news. But what when that gospel was forgotten or distorted?—as it *was* distorted when the emotion induced in the simple multitudes by both the priests and the secular powers was made an emotion of fear.

In the feudal period authority was remote and cruel, and the assumption followed that God's authority must be the same. Henry Adams, in *Mont-Saint-Michel and Chartres*, has made clear how there then grew up "what is in substance a separate religion. . . . what men wanted most in the Middle Ages was not merely law or equity, but also and particularly favour. Strict justice, either on earth or in heaven, was the last thing that society cared to face. . . . like children, they yearned for protection, pardon, and love. This was what the Trinity, though omnipotent, could not give. . . . God could not be love. God was Justice, Order, Unity, Perfection; He could not be human and imperfect, nor could the Son or the Holy Ghost be other than the Father. The Mother alone was human, imperfect, and could love."[4] Therefore the Mother began to be considered the one agency of pity. She must come between the sinner and the wrath of God.

In the religious paintings of the medieval period one sees what had happened to the conception of Christ. He was no more remembered as the "friend of tax collectors and sinners" (Luke 7:34) who had come to seek and to save the lost. Instead, he was pictured as the relentless judge upon his throne, before whose terrible wrath the damned went down to the fires of hell—*unless* some new power in heaven moved him to have pity. And that new power could only be the Mother, exalted by a faith that grew out of human longing to be the Queen of Heaven. So there developed the cult of the Virgin, with the building of cathedrals —like that of Chartres—and innumerable lesser shrines to her predominant honor. And thus it has come about that in Roman Catholic worship the prayer that seems most instinctive among the people is *Ave Maria, ora pro nobis!*

All that is an exaggeration which is possible only when men have forgotten the sufficiency of Christ, and it can come close to an idolatry. No Queen of Heaven is needed to soften a wrathful God. To suppose so is to lose the heart of the gospel which Jesus in his life and in his sacrifice embodied: that "God is love" (I John 4:8) and that "like as a father pities his children" (Ps. 103:13), so the love of God enfolds the least and lowliest of the souls that he has made.

What, then, is the supreme significance for all Christians which the real Mary of Nazareth, the mother of our Lord, will always have? It is not in a mythological conception of her as part of a heavenly pantheon. It is, first, in the fact that although her life moved in a narrow sphere—the same narrow sphere against which many instinctively rebel—it nevertheless found fulfillment there. Her greatness, as Frederick W. Robertson said in one of his never-to-be-forgotten sermons, "was the glory of simple Womanhood; the glory of being true to the nature assigned to her by her Maker; the glory of motherhood; the glory of a 'meek and quiet spirit, which in the sight of God is of great price.' She was not the Queen of Heaven, but she was something nobler still, a creature content to be what God had made her: in unselfishness, and humbleness, and purity, rejoicing in God her Saviour, content that He had regarded the lowliness of His handmaiden."[5]

And the second reason why the life of Mary is forever meaningful is because she shared our human lot in the aspect of it which is most poignant, and in so doing has become the symbol of the truth that it is when a life endures most that it may be most enlarged. Nearly every human being at some time cries out for that faith and hope. To all lives there come the times of darkness. Some heavy calamity falls, involving not only oneself but another life which love is helpless to protect. A mother watches desperately by the bed of her sick child: a father sees his son struck down by some malignant evil which has risen up against him. Then, with all the lights gone out, the agonized desire is to find some candle burning. In the bleak loneliness of suffering, is there a witness to a strength that can come from God?

From the Gospel record this is certain: what Mary had gone through did sound such deeps of suffering as no other human experience could exceed. She had seen her son rejected: at home in Nazareth, and in Jerusalem, the center of the nation's life. She had watched the first excited response of the crowd turn into indifference and then into the mob cruelty that cried out, "Crucify him!" She had stood on the slopes of Calvary and listened to the jeers of those who wanted nothing but to see him die. So she had become the ultimate symbol of the *Mater dolorosa*.

Because she was thus the Mother of Sorrows, there had come true the words which old Simeon had spoken: "A sword will pierce through your own soul also, that thoughts out of many hearts may be revealed" (Luke 2:35). Men and women need to see objectified outside themselves the limitless significance of what they feel and want to trust, but cannot find words with which to justify. Why has this calamity come? What is the meaning of it? How can I ever understand? Questions such as these beset the stricken spirit, and no inward answer comes. But something else may come which is greater than an explicit answer. It is the lifting up of one's own sorrow into contact with some vaster sorrow, in oneness with which there is revealed a depth and dignity of experience which one could not have attained alone. That is why the remembrance of Mary has been a consolation to so many. There in her is revealed the terrible reality of pain, but also the fact that somehow it can be part of the process of redemption.

And Others Less Beneficent

As was noted in the preceding chapter, the world of early centuries was a man's world, and so for the most part was its history. Its conspicuous events were generally events of violence. In its most vivid scenes, including those of the Old Testament, women were not likely to appear. But there were exceptions. If there were no warlike figures quite in the mold of a Boadicea, nevertheless there were women who in the crises of a people's fortunes played their decisive roles.

This present chapter which has to do with some of those women may seem discordant with what has gone before and with what will follow, and such in part it actually is. But discord can accent the main theme. It would be sentimentality to suggest that womanhood is always beautiful. Few if any individuals have in them a flame that is in every respect beneficent. Sometimes it may be devastating. And that in varying degrees was true of three figures in the Old Testament: Deborah of the Book of Judges—vastly different from the Deborah of the Book of Genesis; Jezebel, Queen of Israel and wife of Ahab; and the heroine of the Book of Esther.

Jezebel! Informed thought may stand incredulous at the inclusion of that name. What place has such as Jezebel in a chronicle of women who were good and great? In any positive sense, none. Certainly there was nothing in her that would serve as a beacon for the road on which humanity would want to walk. But in the long gallery of the powerful women of history the portrait of Jezebel cannot be ignored, and to study that portrait is to correct a too facile idea of what womanhood will incessantly represent. Human nature is a strange and diverse thing, and sometimes the qualities which generally are masculine may cross the borderline and become the driving force in a woman's will. In that event it may indeed become true that "the female of the species is deadlier than the male." The story of Jezebel compels attention for its sheer vividness of interest. But more important, the murky flame of her spirit by its contrast makes more admirable the light that is in the better kind of womanhood for which the world is grateful.

Deborah, of the savage era of the Judges, was like Jezebel in this one respect, that she had nothing to do with gentleness. She was capable of acts which would shock a tender conscience, but there was nobility in her purposes. The central figure in the Book of Esther, the young queen from whom the book takes its name, was finer than the other two. Why then should she be linked with them, and especially with Jezebel? Because there was one quality which they all illustrate from different angles: the woman's instinct for unlimited identification with a person or a cause, which can result in good or evil according to the direction in which it turns.

In what was probably the twelfth century B.C. the people of Israel were fighting precariously to consolidate their hold upon the land of Canaan. Moses had inspired the exodus from Egypt, and Joshua had led the tribes across the Jordan River to the capture of Jericho. Little by little the country west of the river was occupied, and the Canaanitish people driven out. But this was far from meaning that the Israelites could now settle down and be secure. There was no central government, and only a loose and shifting impulse among the various tribes to stand together. Around the borders of the country which they had managed to seize were hostile peoples who represented incessant danger: Amorites, Moabites, Midianites, and Bedouin marauders from the deserts in the east. If there were to be any orderly control arising in the midst of the general confusion, it would have to depend upon individuals dominant enough to be natural centers of authority. Such were the persons who gave the name to the Book of Judges; but to understand the term aright one must put out of mind the instinctive modern conception of a dignitary presiding sedately in an established court of law, and visualize instead the individual who by sheer force of personal endowments made the average people turn to him for leadership. Among these so-called "judges" were Gideon and Jephthah, whose exploits as men of war have come down in the hero-stories of the exultant chronicle. But among them was Deborah, whose spirit had an intensity that could set men on fire. In the hill country of Ephraim she saw the tribes of Israel threatened by a powerful rallying of enemies under Jabin, king of Canaan. "She sent and summoned Barak," and she ordered him to "take ten thousand [men] from the tribe of Naphtali and the tribe of Zebulun" and go out to meet the Canaanites. Barak, the rough fighting man, saw in her something that was stronger than an army of ordinary soldiers—the blazing exaltation such as centuries later men would see in a Joan of Arc. "If you will go with me," Barak said, "I will go; but if you will not go with me, I will not go" (Judg. 4:6, 8). Deborah went. There was a great victory. The Canaanitish army was destroyed. Sisera, its commander, fled; and he was killed by Jael, the wife of Heber the Kenite, when he took refuge in her tent.

One of the most magnificent bursts of poetry in the Old Testament is the chant of triumph after the victory which was won, when others had been fearful, by Zebulun

> . . . a people that jeoparded their lives to the death;
> Naphtali too, on the heights of the field (Judg. 5:18).

The whole chant has savage vengeance in it. It belongs to a period when instincts were primitive and unrestrained. But its significance is in the fact that out of the clash and confusion of physical passions there emerges a witness to the power of spirit —the spirit of a woman whose commitment to what she looked upon as a holy cause was so passionate that she had an authority before which men stood in awe.

Deborah of the Book of Judges is to be judged according to the standards of her time. The terrible exultancy of her victory chant that rejoiced in the killing of Sisera must shock a more sensitively developed conscience (though it is not clear that modern consciences are more sensitively developed when it comes to controlling the passions aroused in war). To Deborah, anything seemed justified if it meant the destruction of her people's enemies. Theoretically, at least, our later centuries regard that as barbaric. But actual human beings, in their crowd emotions still not too far from the barbaric, can condone and even glorify terrible things committed in the name of patriotism. That was what Deborah did; and along with her limitations, the greatness which can be in the mixed thing called patriotism did ennoble her. The cause she served was the biggest thing she knew. In her intention, she was on the side of righteousness, and she brought to it everything she had.

After Deborah comes the second of the extraordinary figures to be remembered: Jezebel, the queen of Israel, whose flaming history is in the First Book of the Kings. She was like Deborah in this: She gave herself completely to whatever she espoused. The difference was that what she did espouse was a loyalty so fiercely narrow and so jealously vindictive that all her power turned to evil, and the flame in her that might have given light was dark with smoke.

It was in the ninth century B.C., about the year 870, that Jezebel, the daughter of the king of Tyre, married Ahab, king of Israel. From that time on, until her violent death, she was to move like a firebrand through the history of the kingdom. To begin with, she brought with her an alien worship—baalism. The Baal gods were believed to be the powers that controlled fertility, and therefore the way to get abundant crops in the field and increase of cattle was to give to these gods the proper homage. And the kind of homage proper was to imitate their functions, through sexual excitement which was directly promoted at the Baal shrines. Jezebel brought Baal priests with her into Israel, and it was the corrupting influence of the Baal worship that roused Elijah, the first of the great prophets, to his passionate witness to the God of Sinai and the Ten Commandments.

For Elijah, Jezebel had a hatred that was implacable. The prophet had dared confront her Baal priests, and—according to the exciting story in the First Book of the Kings—humiliated them in a contest on Mt. Carmel and roused the religious passions of the watching crowd to such a point that many of the priests were set upon and slain. Then it was Jezebel who sent her message to Elijah: "So may the gods do to me, and more also, if I do not make your life as the life of one of them by this time tomorrow!" (I Kings 19:2.) Before her fury even Elijah felt his spirit sink. It was as though the dark wrath of this portentous woman had come like an eclipse to swallow up the sun. With his courage for the moment broken, Elijah fled into the desert; and he cried to God, "It is enough; now, O Lord, take away my life; for I am no better than my fathers" (19:4).

Elijah recovered his fortitude, and he came back from the mountain cave where he had hidden himself. Now he would encounter Jezebel again—not directly this time, but in the person of the king whom her stronger purpose dominated. Next to the palace of Ahab was the vineyard of a man named Naboth, and Ahab wanted that vineyard as his own. Naboth would not sell it; and Ahab, vexed and sullen, went and lay down on his bed like a petulant child and would not eat. Not so Jezebel. If Ahab wanted Naboth's vineyard, she would make sure he got it. Who was this nobody who thought he could frustrate a royal wish? She forged letters with Ahab's name and seal, and sent them to the elders and nobles in the city, in which she commanded that Naboth should be seized, exhibited before the people, accused by false witnesses of having blasphemed God and the king, and then taken out and stoned to death. All this was done. Whereupon Jezebel went to Ahab and said to him, "Arise, take possession of the vineyard of Naboth the Jezreelite, which he refused to give you for money; for Naboth is not alive, but dead" (I Kings 21:15).

Jezebel seemed to have triumphed; but the story of course was not finished, and would go on to its grim end. When Ahab went to take possession of the vineyard, there at the gate stood Elijah. The guilty conscience of the king shrank before the awesome figure of the prophet. "Have you found me, O my enemy?" Ahab said; and the prophet answered, "Yes, I have found you, because you have sold yourself to do what is evil in the sight of the Lord" (21:20). Then he pronounced upon Ahab and all his house, and supremely upon Jezebel, the doom that would await them. As he prophesied, so it befell. Ahab, in battle at Ramoth-gilead, was shot by an arrow that pierced the joints of his armor, and he died propped up against his chariot's rail.

So much for Ahab. There remained the part of Elijah's prophecy that had to do with Jezebel. Ahab was succeeded by his son Joram; and Joram was attacked and slain outside his city of Jezreel by the rebel and usurper Jehu. Now Jezebel also was to meet the terrible end which Elijah had foretold—but meet it still defiant. Jehu drove into the city where Jezebel was. Jezebel adorned herself royally and stood upon a balcony, and faced Jehu with her scorn as he looked up from below. "Throw her down," he commanded servants who had come behind her. They did; and as her broken body lay in the road, the dogs devoured her flesh and licked up her blood.

So lived and died Jezebel, who has been called "the Lady Macbeth of the Old Testament"; and aptly, because, with all the differences in detail between their histories, there is a grim likeness in what they were. Each of them had a fierce possessiveness for her husband, so that she was determined that anything he wanted he should have, and she would be the one to see he got it. Macbeth wanted a crown, and so Lady Macbeth instigated the murder of the king; Jezebel, equally merciless for the sake of what Ahab wanted, brought about the killing of the little man who had no defense. Each one had an intensity of purpose that could override all hesitation in her partner. "Art thou afeard," said Lady Macbeth,

To be the same in thine own act and valour
As thou art in desire? . . .
And live a coward in thine own esteem,
Letting "I dare not" wait upon "I would"? . . .
I shame to wear a heart so white.[1]

And Jezebel, scornful of Ahab's hesitation to do away with
Naboth, exclaims, "Do you now govern Israel? Arise, and eat
bread, and let your heart be cheerful; I will give you the vineyard of Naboth the Jezreelite" (I Kings 21:7).

Moreover, of the two, Jezebel could maintain a sovereign
consistency of evil courage which even the great figure in Shakespeare's tragedy could not match. In Lady Macbeth there was
enough of conscience to rise up at last and haunt her and drive
her mad. Walking in her sleep, she cries, "Here's the smell of the
blood still: all the perfumes of Arabia will not sweeten this little
hand."[2] But nothing ever broke the proud consistency of Jezebel. She died, as she had lived, uncompromising and undaunted.
Her loyalties were terrible in that they were linked with evil;
but there was grandeur in their revelation of the intensity of
purpose that can burn in a woman's heart.

In order to understand the third figure in the present com-
parison it is important to remember the story and the historical
background of the Old Testament book in which she is the
center.

In 586 B.C. Nebuchadnezzar had besieged and captured Jerusalem, and carried away most of the Jewish people as captive
exiles to Babylon. There they remained until 536 B.C. when
Babylon in its turn was invested, its vast walls and defences
breached, and the city sacked and reduced to ruins by a new
conqueror, Cyrus. For two hundred years, until Alexander the
Great and his Macedonian phalanxes began their march into
Asia, the country which had been the Babylonian empire was
under the rule of Persia. Though a few of the Jewish exiles were
permitted to make their painful way back to what had been
their homeland, the great bulk of them were in the regions to

which their ancestors had been brought. For the most part they were decently treated by the Persian kings, but they were still an alien and a subject people.

The story of the Book of Esther is laid in Susa, the Persian capital, "in the days of Ahasuerus, the Ahasuerus who reigned from India to Ethiopia over one hundred and twenty-seven provinces" (1:1). Ahasuerus gives a great banquet for his nobles; and in the midst of it, when his heart "was merry with wine" (1:10) he sends for Vashti, his queen. She refuses to appear; at which the King is enraged, the more particularly because there were whisperings that "this deed of the queen will be made known to all women, causing them to look with contempt upon their husbands, since they will say, 'King Ahasuerus commanded Queen Vashti to be brought before him, and she did not come'" (1:17). Therefore he divorced her; and the next thing was to get himself another wife.

The command went out, "Let beautiful young virgins be sought out for the king" (2:2). Many were brought, and among them one who was "beautiful and lovely" (2:7). Her name was Esther. When Ahasuerus saw her, "she found grace and favor in his sight" (2:17). He determined to make her his queen; and this he did. Now Esther was a Jewess, but Ahasuerus did not know it.

In the kingdom the man at court who was in highest favor was a man named Haman. This was so well recognized that all others at the court, obviously on the lookout for their own advantage, bowed down and made obeisance when Haman passed by. But Mordecai, a Jew, stood stiff and unbending. At that, Haman's offended vanity swelled up as with the poison of a puffed adder. He hated this Mordecai; he would have revenge not only on him, but on all his people. He said to King Ahasuerus, "There is a certain people scattered abroad and dispersed . . . in all the provinces of your kingdom; their laws are different from those of every other people, and they do not keep the king's laws, so that it is not for the king's profit to tolerate them" (3:8).

Haman's craftiness so beguiled the dull-witted king that he

signed a decree, to go out to all the provinces, that on a certain day all Jews, young and old, should be set upon and slain. Then "the king and Haman sat down to drink" (3:15).

Now came the moment when Esther was to take the central role. Mordecai sent a messenger to her, who begged her in Mordecai's name to go to Ahasuerus where he sat in his audience hall, and plead with him to reverse the decree which Haman had procured. Her terrible dilemma was that to make such appeal would be to reveal in one sudden moment to the capricious king what he had not known: that she herself was a Jewess. Moreover, to go into the king's presence without being summoned was accounted a presumption that might be punished by the subject's execution—and she had not been summoned.

She sent back to Mordecai the pathetic message of her fear. How could she dare to do what he had asked? But neither could she fail to recognize the awful pressure which was upon her nevertheless. "Think not that in the king's palace you will escape any more than all the other Jews," said Mordecai. "For if you keep silence at such a time as this, relief and deliverance will rise for the Jews from another quarter, but you and you father's house will perish. And who knows whether you have not come to the kingdom for such a time as this?"

There was nothing left for Esther but to yield. She besought Mordecai to gather all the Jewish people and to hold a fast. She and her maids would fast also. "Then I will go to the king, though it is against the law; and if I perish, I perish" (4:13-16).

She did go in to Ahasuerus, in her royal robes. Unpredictable as always, the king was captivated this time by her appearance. What was her request, he asked. Then she made adroit reply. The throne room, she realized, was no place in which to voice her intimate appeal. So what she asked was this: Would the king and Haman come to dinner in the queen's apartment? Yes, the king would come, and Haman too.

From that point the story moves on through its astonishing sequence.

Haman was filled with exultation. He went home, gathered his friends, and to them and to his wife "he recounted . . . all the promotions with which the king had honored him, and how he had advanced him above the princes and the servants of the king." And then he added, "Even Queen Esther let no one come with the king to the banquet she prepared but myself. And tomorrow also I am invited by her together with the king" (5:11-12). And filled now with overweening confidence that everything he had wanted was opening up before him, he went out and ordered a gallows to be built—a gallows on which presently he would hang Mordecai the Jew.

But the denouement for him was to come with shocking difference. Ahasuerus had suddenly been reminded that it was Mordecai who a short while before, by discovering a plot, had saved the king from assassination, and nothing yet had been done to reward him. Ahasuerus' mind was filled with that, and the next morning he asked his servants, "Who is in the court?" "Haman," they answered; and the king said, "Let him come in." (Now what Haman had come for was to ask the king's permission for the hanging of Mordecai on the gallows he was having made; and he had not the faintest notion of what he was to hear.)

"What ought to be done for a man whom the king wants to honor?" Ahasuerus asked. He means me, Haman thought; but of course he must give no sign that he thought so. He would make his answer sound like the impersonal suggestion properly responsive to the king's question. So he outlined elaborately what would be the highest honor the king could give. Very well, the king said; that was the way the honor should be given—to Mordecai! And Haman should carry it out. Haman should see to it that Mordecai was arrayed in royal robes and seated on the king's horse; and Haman should lead the horse with Mordecai on it through the city and proclaim that this was done by the king's decree.

Nor was that all. At the queen's banquet the desperate Haman heard himself accused by Esther of having treacherously denounced the Jews; and when in his terror he flung himself on Esther's couch beseeching her, the furious king called his ser-

vants to cover Haman's face and carry him out, and hang him
on the gallows he had built for Mordecai.

Commentators on the Old Testament have tried to link the
story of Esther with the known facts of Persian history, with
conjectures that the Artaxerxes of the story may have been
Xerxes I (485-465 B.C.) or Artaxerxes II (404-358 B.C.). But
there has been no success in the search for evidence that there
actually was a queen named Esther. It seems more probable that
the book is a historical romance, written perhaps in the second
century B.C. at the time of the persecution under Antiochus
Epiphanes, to voice for the Jewish people the passionate conviction of their divinely given destiny which flamed in the
heroic Maccabean wars. Whatever may have been the origin
of the book, and whatever be the measure large or small of its
detailed conformity to history, it dramatizes two realities which
are timeless.

One is the mighty fact of the permanence of the Jewish
people, this people of the Covenant, moving indestructible
through centuries of persecution, as on an eternal road. It is no
wonder that to Jews the Book of Esther is precious, and that
it is read every year at the Festival of Purim, for it embodies
their flaming faith in the God of the patriarchs and the prophets who had chosen them for His own, and against whose
sustaining power no evil forces can prevail.

And the second reality is the everlasting strength that may
be in a woman's seeming weakness. Esther shrank from her
perilous commission. All she could say was, "I will go; and if
I perish, I perish." But the great fact was that she did go. She
would represent once more the woman's selflessness, which in
moments of crisis is capable of the decisive courage; and which
in all the ordinary hours of life can be a redeeming light.

III

Joan of Arc

If the story of Joan of Arc were not certified history, it would be accounted as exaggerated fiction. A peasant girl appearing as it seemed from nowhere, winning the reluctant notice of warriors and noblemen, putting herself at the head of armies, driving back the enemies of her humiliated country, crowning a king, burned as a heretic and afterward canonized as a saint— could this be actual fact? Yet fact it was, and the wonder of it stands as one of the everlasting mysteries of the human spirit.

That mystery is all the greater when it is contrasted with the extraordinarily full and specific knowledge we possess of the outward framework of Joan's career: the circumstances of her childhood, the choices she made, the things she did, the impression she made upon a host of people. When she had been captured by her enemies and had been put on trial for her life, her relentless examiners searched every aspect of her life and day after day demanded her replies. The official Latin record of that trial, preserved among the archives of France, was rescued by the research scholar Quicherat a century ago from what might have been oblivion, and now is available in French and English translations for all who choose to read. Moreover, in 1455, twenty-four years after Joan had been condemned and burned at the stake, a court of lawyers and ecclesiastics convened by the order of Pope Calixtus reviewed her original trial. Before this court were summoned many of those still living who had known Joan of Arc; peasant neighbors in the village where she had been born, soldiers who had fought with her, men and women of Orléans and other cities where Joan had been, priests who were at Rouen at the time of her trial, some of whom had heard her witness before her judges and had seen her when judgment was pronounced against her and she was led out to die. Their testimony, given under oath, has the startling directness of intimate knowledge; so that listening to their words, it is as though one were carried back five centuries and made a part of that actual world in which Joan of Arc was a living and breathing force.

She was born—this Jeanne d'Arc whose name we have anglicized into Joan—in the little village of Domremy-la-Pucelle, in Lorraine. According to the most probable evidence, her birthday was January 6, 1412. Her father, Jacques d'Arc, was a peasant farmer, steady and industrious, and well regarded by his neighbors, so that he more than once held minor official posts in the affairs of Domremy and in its relation to the villages round about. Both the father and mother had the simple inherited piety that centered in the church and the priest and the confessional; and it was her mother, Joan said, who taught her the Lord's Prayer, the creed, and the Ave Maria. Concerning Joan herself, Isabellette, the wife of a laborer, testified at the hearing in 1455:

> From my childhood I knew the parents of Jeannette; as to Jeannette, I knew her in my youth and as long as she remained with her parents. She was very hospitable to the poor, and would even sleep on the hearth in order that the poor might lie in her bed. She was not fond of playing, at which we, her companions, complained. She liked work; and would spin, labour with her father, look after the house, and sometimes mind the sheep. She was never seen idling in the roads; she was more often in Church at prayer.[1]

Something like that, no doubt, might have been true of other young girls in the obscure little villages of fifteenth-century

France. To go about the everyday duties of the house and the field, to go to church, to be kind and hospitable, might make someone affectionately remembered by the neighbors; but in that fact alone there is certainly no hint of the emergence of a figure who can never be forgotten as long as history is told. In order to grasp—or to begin to grasp—the significance of what came out of Domremy it is necessary to recall what was happening in the whole of France and to ponder the unique and ineffable echo which those happenings woke in one girl's mind and soul.

Since 1339 France had been torn by the Hundred Years' War. Ever since 1066, when William of Normandy as William the Conqueror had made himself king of England, the English kings had claimed and held sovereignty over provinces in France: Normandy first, and later others added to it. In England the royal power had been exercised with such authority that the country had been welded into effective unity; in France there was the continual threat of great feudal lords whose armed forces stood in the way of any unifying rule. Consequently the English penetration of France expanded. A century after William the Conqueror, Henry II of England possessed not only Normandy and Brittany, but Anjou and Maine and Aquitaine, more than half of the territory of France. Edward III (1327-77) carried his armies across the channel for the beginning of the Hundred Years' War, and routed the French chivalry in the battles of Crecy and Poitiers. Then in 1415 Henry V won the crushing victory of Agincourt, and this time it seemed that the very existence of France as an independent realm was in mortal jeopardy. By the Treaty of Troyes in 1420, it was determined that Henry V should marry Katherine, the daughter of Charles VI of France; and at the death of Charles should succeed to the throne of France, united thus with that of England. Two years later Henry V died, leaving a nine-month-old son to carry on as Henry VI—under regents who governed for him during his infancy—his father's claim to be sovereign of France. The son of Charles VI, a weak youth of nineteen, was ignored in the Treaty of Troyes as of no account, but those among the French nobles who still resisted English rule saw in him, the Dauphin, the only rallying point for the future of France; and their armed forces kept possession of such territory as they could hold. It was not much. The Dauphin himself, who claimed to be Charles VII, but had never been crowned, took refuge within the walls of the castle of Chinon. Orléans and other cities in the valley of the Loire were loyal to his cause; but all the north of France was held by the English and by the forces of the Duke of Burgundy, who had allied himself with England.

Such was the condition of her country when the young girl whom her neighbors knew just as the peasant daughter of Jacques d'Arc was growing up in Domremy: a country invaded by a foreign army, and split by bitter rivalries and factions within itself. Although Domremy lay almost at the border of France, it was not out of reach of the ruinous civil war. A raiding party of the adherents of the Duke of Burgundy descended on the village, stripped the fields and burned the church as a lesson to the people of Domremy, most of whom were known to favor the Dauphin. In that general fact Joan was like her neighbors. But in the intensity of her spirit she was different. To her the Dauphin's cause was no matter of lukewarm preference. It represented to her the soul of France; and because it did so, the loyalty which among the general run of people might have seemed only accidental became instead a religious passion.

Then began the facts which in their immense results are written large in history, but before which any trivial attempt at explanation stands halted and hushed: Joan's visions and her Voices:

> I was thirteen [she said] when I had a Voice from God for my help and guidance. The first time that I heard this Voice, I was very much frightened; it was midday, in the summer, in my father's garden. . . . It

seemed to me to come from lips I should reverence. When I heard it for the third time, I recognized that it was the Voice of an Angel. This Voice has always guarded me well, and I have always understood it; it instructed me to be good, and to go often to Church. . . . It said to me two or three times a week: "You must go into France." . . . I could stay no longer. It said to me, "Go, raise the siege which is being made before the City of Orléans. Go," it added, "to Robert de Baudricourt, Captain of Vaucouleurs: he will furnish you with an escort to accompany you." And I replied that I was but a poor girl who knew nothing of riding or fighting.[2]

"A poor girl who knew nothing of riding or fighting"; and yet to her what seemed a divine command that she should go and offer herself as the deliverer of a beleaguered country. What bringing together of opposite realities could have seemed more irrational than that? Nevertheless, what might have been most incredible did actually come to pass. The peasant girl of Domremy did become the Maid of France, rallying and inspiring its demoralized armies, raising the siege of Orléans, driving back the English, taking the otherwise helpless Dauphin to the cathedral at Reims and having him crowned king.

The Voice that came to her first, said Joan, "was Saint Michael. I saw him before my eyes; he was not alone, but quite surrounded by the Angels of Heaven."[3] Later were revealed to her two saints who were to be her special counselors and comforters: St. Catherine and St. Margaret. To many—even in religious circles—those names may carry now no clear identity; but in medieval France, where the instinctive and naïve piety of simple people absorbed without question the teaching of an undivided church, St. Catherine and St. Margaret were revered as two of the most sure and certain intercessors in a heaven that was more real than most of the things of earth. According to tradition, Margaret, in Asia Minor at the beginning of the fourth century, had been converted to Christianity and disowned by her pagan father. Tending sheep in the fields, her beauty excited the lust of a Roman prefect. When she repulsed him, he caused her to be arrested and condemned as a Christian; and after she had been martyred, she became the patron saint of virgins, and Joan may have knelt in the village church before the statue of a shepherdess leading a chained dragon, the statue of St. Margaret. Catherine also belonged to the fourth century in the time of the Roman emperor Maximinus, before whom it was said that she dared to appear and denounce him for his persecution of the Christians. She too was martyred, and her symbol was the wheel of the torture rack which her persecutors tried to use against her. So there was appropriateness, both gallant and wistful, in Joan's reaching out toward these two virgin saints as she felt her maidenhood called to an adventure that was full of deadly hazard.

As to the whole fact of her belief in her visions and her Voices, none may dare to speak with dogmatism. The angelic forms which she said she saw before her eyes, and the words she heard, may seem inexplicable except as the projection of immense emotions wakened in her soul. But although the form of what she held to be her revelations goes beyond our little understanding, who can stop short of reverent acknowledgment that there did come to her out of the Infinite a spiritual Reality beyond our mortal compass, bringing to her the superhuman illumination and courage which alone could have made possible the unparalleled things she was about to do?

"Go into France! Go to Robert de Baudricourt, Captain of Vaucouleurs,"[4] the Voice had said. Her father, she knew, would think that to be only madness. But at the beginning, as afterward, her mystical beliefs that seemed unearthly were linked with a practical intelligence which could find the plain roads that led to the ends she had to reach. A cousin of hers was married to Durand Laxart, who lived in a village near Vaucouleurs. She went to him, and appealed to him to go with her to Robert de Baudricourt. He did escort her, persuaded—against who can say what initial reluctance and incredulity?—by the passionate conviction of this girl whom he, like others afterward, could not long resist. But Robert de Baudricourt was of tougher sort. He thought this preposterous child from Domremy was out of her wits. "Take her back to her father and tell him to box her ears," he said.[5]

But the next spring there at his door was Joan again. This time Joan won the attention of two of his lieutenants, Jean de Metz, and Bertrand de Poulengey. Now, to his astonishment, de Baudricourt himself began to listen. Hard-bitten soldier though he was, he lived in an age when belief in the miraculous was familiar. Perhaps he had better cross himself before what might be coming as a miracle in this girl. After all, the Dauphin's cause had grown so desperate that no reasonable measures were likely to save it. Joan wanted to go where the Dauphin was. Well, let her go then. He himself would be rid of her; and as to what might happen next, he could wait and see.

So he gave permission for Jean de Metz and Bertrand de Poulengey to take Joan to the Dauphin's castle at Chinon— provided they could get there across the three hundred and fifty miles of intervening country, over winter roads that might be blocked at any point by brigands or by marauding troops of the Duke of Burgundy. On February 23, 1429, late in the afternoon, Joan and her escorts rode out of the gates of Vaucouleurs. Concerning that journey to Chinon we are not left to speculation. Jean de Metz, testifying at the inquiry ordered by Pope Calixtus in 1455, told in his own words of how he had first seen Joan in Vaucouleurs, of how they fared on the roads to Chinon, and—most important—of the effect Joan had had upon him.

> When Jeannette was at Vaucouleurs, I saw her in a
> red dress, poor and worn; she lived at the house of one
> named Henri Leroyer. "What are you doing here?" I

said to her. "Must the king* be driven from the kingdom; and are we to be English?" "I am come here," she answered me, "to this royal town to speak to Robert de Baudricourt, to the end that he may conduct me or have me conducted to the king; but Robert cares neither for me nor for my words. Nevertheless, before the middle of Lent I must be with the king. . . . No one in the world—neither kings, nor dukes, nor any others —can recover the kingdom of France; there is no succor to be expected save from me; but, nevertheless, I would rather spin with my poor mother—for this is not my proper estate: it is, however, necessary that I should go, and do this because my Lord wills that I should do it." And when I asked her who this Lord was, she told me it was God. Then I pledged my faith to her, touching her hand, and promised that, with God's guidance, I would conduct her to the king. I asked her when she wished to start. "Sooner at once than tomorrow, and sooner tomorrow than later," she said. I asked her if she could make this journey, dressed as she was. She replied that she would willingly take a man's dress. Then I gave her the dress and equipment of one of my men. Afterwards, the inhabitants of Vaucouleurs had a man's dress made for her, with all the necessary requisites; I also procured for her a horse. . . . We travelled for the most part at night, for fear of the Burgundians and the English, who were masters of the roads. We journeyed eleven days, always riding toward the said town of Chinon. On the way, I asked her many times if she would really do all she said. "Have no fear," she answered us, "what I am commanded to do, I will do. . . . my Lord—that is God—told me that I must go and fight in order to re-

---

* By "the king" both Jean de Metz and Joan refer to Charles who was then only the Dauphin, for he had not yet been crowned or acknowledged as sovereign of France. W. R. B.

gain the Kingdom of France." On the way, Bertrand
and I slept every night by her—Jeanne being at my
side, fully dressed. She inspired me with such respect
that for nothing in the world would I have dared to
molest her; also, never did I feel toward her—I say it
on oath—any carnal desire. On the way she always
wished to hear mass. She said to us: "If we can, we shall
do well to hear mass." But for fear of being recognized,
we were only able to hear it twice. I had absolute faith
in her. Her words and her ardent faith in God in-
flamed me. I believed she was sent from God.[6]

And Bertrand de Poulengey was moved by her in the same
way as was Jean de Metz. He said:

We were eleven days on the road during which we
had many anxieties. But Jeanne told us always that
we had nothing to fear, and that, once arrived at
Chinon, the noble Dauphin would show us good countenance. I felt myself inspired by her words, but I
saw that she was indeed a messenger of God. Never
did I see in her any evil.[7]

The "noble Dauphin" from whom Joan trusted that she
would have "good countenance" was actually far short of being
noble. He was a poor shifty creature, humiliated by the Treaty
of Troyes, and under the shadow of the fact that his own
mother had cast doubt on his legitimacy and therefore his
right to the crown. But to Joan, who had never seen him, he
was not yet the disillusioning actuality; he was the royal symbol of the spirit of beleaguered France. She clothed him with
the mystical glamour of her own ideal.

She needed determination and tough purpose to keep on
doing so in face of what she encountered when she arrived at
the castle of Chinon. Among the Dauphin's retinue there had
been a buzz of mocking speculation about this woman whom
Robert de Baudricourt had said he was sending. Here was a

chance for sport; a chance to see whether this incredible would-be deliverer could be made ridiculous. So it was arranged that one of the courtiers should pretend to be the Dauphin, while the Dauphin mingled in the crowd.

Then occurred the event (to be followed by others also) which manifested in this peasant girl an intuition, a clairvoyance, a supernatural illumination—call it what we may—that goes beyond any smooth explaining. V. Sackville West, in *Saint Joan of Arc*, summing up the sworn depositions made later by some who were at Chinon that day, describes what happened thus:

> She was to be received in the Grande Salle, a splendid apartment on the upper floor of the Château du Milieu, some seventy feet long by twenty-five feet wide, with a vast hooded fireplace at one end, three large windows overlooking the gardens of the inner court, and one smaller window overlooking the town, the river, and the landscape beyond. Curiosity had filled the *salle*, into which Jeanne was introduced by the Comte de Vendôme. . . . The hall was lit by fifty torches and packed with over three hundred people, a brilliant crowd of soldiers, courtiers, and prelates, some of them hostile, some of them frivolously amused; but all of them curious to see this new exhibit who might for an hour at least enliven the farce of their existence in a Court which was a Court only in name.[8]

Joan looked about her, first at the courtier pretending to be the Dauphin and seated at the place of honor. Then turning to scan the crowd, she went up directly to the real Dauphin; half hidden by others who were placed in front of him, and thus addressed him:

"Gentil Dauphin, j'ai nom Jehanne la Pucelle.
The King of Heaven sends me to you with the message

that you shall be anointed and crowned in the city of
Reims, and that you shall be the lieutenant of the King
of Heaven, who is King of France." . . .

This small, queer, solitary figure. . . showed no sign
of hesitation, distress, shyness, or embarrassment, ad-
dressing the Dauphin familiarly and without awe, in
terms of a firm arrogance which could not be called
boastful in view of its sincerity and simplicity. One
wonders especially what the Archbishop of Reims
thought, being present, on hearing these arrangements
made for his own cathedral, to which, in spite of having been Archbishop of Reims for over twenty years,
he had never yet paid a visit. Prelates of that standing
were not accustomed to hearing of coronations arranged for them by unknown peasants; coronations
either came, or did not come, according to the great
traditional hierarchy of France. Still the Dauphin held
firm and prolonged the test. "It is not I who am the
King, Jehanne. *There* is the King," he said, pointing
to one of his lords. She was not to be taken in. "In
God's name, noble prince, it is you and none other."[9]

The Dauphin had delayed for two days after Joan had arrived at Chinon before he had let her come into his presence.
When she had recognized him notwithstanding the shabby
effort to mislead her, he could not help being to some degree
impressed. But he was still irresolute as to what to do. Joan,
with her burning conviction of being under the guidance of
God, moved forward with single purpose toward her goal.
But Charles the Dauphin, a small man faced with big issues,
halted between half-superstitious belief and fear that any belief
he showed might seem absurd. What he did was to delay again,
and cast about for somebody else to be responsible for the next
decision. He sent Joan to Poitiers, to be examined by a panel
of ecclesiastics presided over by the Archbishop of Reims. Two
years later, when Joan at Rouen was on trial for her life, she

demanded again and again that the proceedings at Poitiers might be read for her defense; but her prosecutors ignored her appeal; those records and their testimony were concealed or perhaps destroyed, and not to this day have they been re- covered. But one person who was at Poitiers, Frère Seguin, a Carmelite and professor of theology, did testify in 1455 as to what happened there. As one of the examiners, "he then in- formed her that God was not willing that they should believe her on her mere word, and that they would not advise the Dauphin to supply her with men-at-arms unless she could give them some proof that she was deserving of their trust. At this point, Jeanne seems to have lost her temper. 'By God's name,' she said, 'I have not come to Poitiers to perform signs. Lead me to Orléans, and I will show you the signs for which I am sent.' "[10]

Four things she made bold to promise. If the Dauphin would give her fighting men to lead, she would lift the siege of Orléans which then was invested by an English army; she would crown the Dauphin at Reims; bring the city of Paris back to its allegiance; and recover the Duke of Orléans, who was a pri- soner in England. One of the examiners, superciliously thinking he could outwit her, said "You say your voices tell you that God wishes to free the people of France from their present calamities. But if He wishes to free them, it is not necessary to have an army." To which Joan replied, "In God's name, the men-at-arms will fight, and God will give the victory!"[11]

When the hearing was completed "we decided," said Frère Seguin, "that, in view of the imminent necessity and of the danger of Orléans, the King might allow the girl to help him and might send her to Orléans."[12] In such terms of patronizing condescension, then, was Joan started on her way; but she her- self was too engrossed in her mission to be concerned with bad manners. Moreover, there were others ready to adventure with her who had none of the sour caution of the ecclesiastics.

At Chinon one of those who had been excited by her spirit was the gay and handsome young Duke of Alençon, who had married the daughter of the Duke of Orléans. He gave Joan a horse, and watched with admiration the way she rode and tilted with a lance. He took her to stay with his wife; and when the young duchess made plain to Joan her reluctance to have her husband go off to more fighting Joan answered, "Madame, fear nothing. I will bring him back to you as safe and well as he is now, or even better."[13]

Now the long delay in the wings was over, and Joan moved out into that almost incredible drama in the arena of history to which her Voices had given their unvaried prompting. The Dauphin decided—or the slow pressure of critical necessity made the decision for him—that Joan should be allowed to go to the relief of Orléans. That way, he thought, there was at least a chance of something miraculous happening. Without that, nothing seemed likely except that the English would conquer the rest of France.

He assembled the few thousand men-at-arms who were available, with commanders who had had some experience in war. He gave Joan a suit of armor, two heralds, and personal attendants. And as she rode out from Chinon she carried a white banner, embroidered with fleur-de-lys, and with a representation of the Lord Christ, holding the world in His hands.

If the siege of Orléans was to be lifted and the English driven back both there and elsewhere, two things were needed: military skill and new inspiration. The aura of romantic wonder which had gathered round the figure of Joan has put its spell upon some historians, so that they see in her, and in her alone, the one who furnished both. She is thought of not only as a spur and challenge, but as the actual commander of all the armies of France, and directing them with "a skill and judgment worthy of the greatest commanders, indeed of Napoleon himself, . . . in two short months accomplishing more than Caesar or Augustus accomplished in so much time."[14] The actual facts were not so sweeping as that—though still beyond all ordinary measurement. Joan did have in military matters a bold intuition born of her belief that she had been given a divine commission, and a flash of genius in recognizing opportunities that conventional military minds were slow to see. The Duke of Alençon said of her, "She was a very simple young girl; but for warlike things—bearing the lance, assembling an army, ordering military operations, directing artillery—she was most skilful."[15] And another of the commanders who fought in her company was astonished at her "many marvelous manoeuvers which had not been thought of by two or three accomplished generals working together."[16] But the fact remains that tactics and strategy were not her supreme contribution. What she did supremely bring to the deliverance of France was the fire of her spirit, and a conviction of divine appointment so passionate that rough men around her were lifted above themselves and filled with a kind of holy awe.

When Joan started from Chinon with the troops that had been assembled, she sent to the Earl of Bedford, the regent in France of the English king, a message which must have made that noble lord for the moment speechless with astonished indignation: "Deliver the keys of all the good towns you have taken and violated in France to the Maid . . . who has been sent by God the King of Heaven." Otherwise, she would come to visit him to his "great detriment."[17] She did also what must have created equal astonishment in another quarter. She ordered that all the disreputable women who had followed the troops should be got rid of, and that all the army should go to mass. Moreover, she was obeyed; because she believed, and in that blazing fact made others willing to believe, that she was the mouthpiece of God.

On Friday, April 29, 1429, the word spread in besieged Orléans that relief was coming. The English had their forts around part of the walled city, but on the east side the cordon of these was thin. Also below the city on the south flowed the river Loire. The commander of the French troops in Orléans was the illegitimate son of the Duke of Orléans, an intrepid fighter who was known, and in the blunt language of the time unabashedly spoken of, as the Bastard. He had planned to send troops from the south of the river upstream in barges to take the English on their relatively unprotected flank; but the wind had been blowing continuously from the east, and the barges could not move against it. Joan arrived at the river. Suddenly, inexplicably, the wind changed. A miracle! the Bastard thought. The troops which had come with Joan, and the cattle and other supplies for the hungry city which they had escorted, would follow; but the Bastard persuaded Joan to cross the river first, and enter one of the gates of Orléans which was opened for her. She did so, and rode through the streets of Orléans where the exultant people surged around her, touching her horse, her armor, her banner, as though she were an angel come from God.

In the next week, with reinforcements arriving for the French, several of the English redoubts were taken, but Orléans was still besieged. Now came the decisive struggle. The strongest bastion held by the English was the fortified stone bridge across the Loire, the Tourelles. Joan insisted that it be attacked. The assault was launched, and all day the fighting raged: on scaling ladders lifted against the tower walls, hand to hand with leaden maces, battle axes, hatchets. At eight o'clock in the evening it seemed that the attack had failed, and Joan herself had been wounded by an arrow between her neck and shoulder; but "she continued none the less to fight, taking no remedy for her wound." The Bastard was about to abandon the assault, but "the maid then came to me, praying me to wait yet a little longer. Thereupon she mounted her horse, retired to a vineyard, all alone by herself, remained in prayer about half an hour, then, returning and seizing her banner by both hands, she placed herself on the edge of the trench. At sight of her the English trembled, and were seized with sudden fear; our people, on the contrary, took courage and began to mount and assail the Tourelles."[18] When darkness fell the fight was over, and the flames from the burning bridge and the broken towers streamed up like a torch of victory into the night.

Shortly thereafter the English lifted the siege of Orléans and retreated. Joan and the French pressed on to further victories and the deliverance of other cities which the English had held.

Then at last she reached the summit of her desires. She took the Dauphin to Reims; and there with the ancient pageantry of the kings of France, he was crowned as Charles VII.

What needed then to be done was to recapture Paris. But the king's timidity and the craft of the Duke of Burgundy frustrated that. Joan set out instead to try to drive the English from Compiegne. Then disaster struck. Cut off outside the drawbridge of the city by superior forces, she was pulled from her horse and captured, and presently sold to the Earl of Bedford. The woman whom he regarded as a witch was in his hands.

Now began the final tragic chapter of the Maid's career. Taken to Rouen, she was put on trial not as a political prisoner, but—through the complicity of Cauchon, the Bishop of Beauvais —for alleged offenses against the church. Her inquisitors tried to make her abjure her Voices, and confess that her victories were the work of witchcraft. They said that she had sinned against her womanhood when she had worn armor and a man's dress. Day by day they brought her from the cell where she was guarded by common English soldiers into the hall where her examiners sat. They browbeat her with incessant questionings. They brought in the executioner to show her the instruments of torture. They demanded her submission as a daughter of the church, bound on pain of heresy to listen to those wiser than herself. Some of her examiners were honest men, trying— within the dreadful limits of their iron preconceptions—to save her soul. They believed that truth was bound up in an institution and its authority. This one intrepid girl who stood before them dared believe that truth can come, like a flame from heaven, straight to the individual soul.

"Do you not then believe," they asked her, "that you are subject to the Church of God which is on earth, that is to say, to our Lord the Pope, to the Cardinals, the Archbishops, Bishops and other prelates of the Church?"

"Yes, I believe myself to be subject to them, but God must be served first," she answered.

"If you will not believe in the Church, if you will not believe that Article of the Creed, 'The Church, One, Holy, Catholic,' you will be declared a heretic, and by other judges punished with the pains of fire."

"I believe that the Church militant cannot err or fail," she said, "but as to my words and deeds, I submit them and refer them all to God, who caused me to do what I have done. . . . I refer me to God thereupon, and to my own self."[19]

No wonder that George Bernard Shaw, in the Preface to *Saint Joan*, could speak of Joan as not only "the most notable Warrior Saint in the Christian calendar" but as "in fact one of the first Protestant martyrs"; because in her there spoke the invincible "protest of the individual soul against the interference of priest or peer between the private man and his God."[20] Through that channel of the illumined single soul—and sometimes through that alone—may come the light by which the church and all its institutions can be purified and redeemed.

Day after day Joan was brought back to be examined, counseled, exhorted, threatened. At length she could stand no more. Yes, she would sign what they told her to sign. She would recant. In her lonely agony, it seemed that perhaps her Voices had misled her. Let her go back to Domremy and forget all that she had tried to do!

So she had abjured and was no longer subject to the ultimate punishment, her judges said. "But because thou hast sinned rashly against God and Holy Church, we condemn thee, finally, definitely, and for salutary penance . . . to perpetual imprisonment, with the bread of sorrow and the water of affliction."[21]

That was what Joan heard, and all her soul flamed up in outrage and defiance. So this was the judgment of the church! It was for this that they had made her sign her recantation! She repudiated now all that they had driven her to say at the moment of her weakness. It was her Voices and not the voice of the church that had been true. She would go to her death proclaiming it.

As a relapsed heretic, her judges now delivered her "to the secular arm"—which meant that they gave her over to the

English who had been waiting for the burning of one they believed to be a witch, who had troubled them too long. Near the church of St. Ouen the stake had been prepared. Joan was led to it, the fagots piled about her, and the fire lighted.

In *Saint Joan* the horror and yet the high triumph of the death of Joan are expressed through one of the figures in Shaw's drama. What he says reflects what actually happened there in Rouen five centuries ago. The English chaplain, who had been most vehement in his denunciation of Joan when she was tried, is shocked almost to madness when he actually sees her burned. Rushing in where the Earl of Warwick was waiting to hear that the execution was complete, the chaplain falls on his knees and cries: "O Christ, deliver me from this fire that is consuming me! She cried to Thee in the midst of it: Jesus! Jesus! Jesus! She is in Thy bosom; and I am in hell forever-more. . . . A soldier gave her two sticks tied together. Thank God he was an Englishman! I might have done it; but I did not: I am a coward, a mad dog, a fool! . . .

"Some of the people laughed at her. They would have laughed at Christ."[22]

❧ IV ❧

Susanna Wesley

One of the great preachers of the late nineteenth century, when he was a young man in college, was asked what he meant to choose as his life work. He answered: "I know what I have thought I would be, but I am beginning to believe that my mother will pray me into the ministry." He did ultimately become a minister, with a joyous fullness of dedication that made him an inspiring force in his world and time. That would not have been possible unless there had been in himself an instinctive response; but it was his mother's intuition and his mother's influence that kindled the hidden possibility into flame.

The same has been true in the relation of other mothers to their sons. Back of St. Augustine was his mother, Monica. Monica was always a Christian, while Augustine, as a young man, wandered off into alien philosophies and led in private a life of which afterward he was bitterly ashamed. Always, as he wrote in his *Confessions*, his mother was begging of God "not gold or silver, nor any mutable or passing good, but the salvation of her son's soul." When, deceiving her, he had left home in North Africa and gone to Italy, she came to him, "resolute through piety, following me over sea and land, in all perils confiding in Thee." When at length he was converted and he told his mother, "she rejoiceth . . . and triumpheth, and blesseth Thee, *Who art able to do above that which we ask or think;* for she perceived that Thou hadst given her more for me, than she was wont to beg."[1] When Monica fell ill at Ostia, and she knew that she would die outside her own land, she and Augustine held long converse on this life and the life to come. "Son," she said to him, "I have no further delight in anything in this life . . . now that my hopes in this world are accomplished."[2] All that she had longed for had been fulfilled in Augustine, and God had answered her prayer that he might completely become His servant.

Few men have made an impact upon their time equal to that of John Wesley; Wesley, who in his evangelism reached out to touch the souls of the neglected and depraved, who brought to the whole society of eighteenth-century England a moral challenge which rebuked the laxity into which its life had fallen, and who created in Methodism a new religious fellowship which sought to bring back the fervor of early Christianity to a dull and complacent church. All this John Wesley did; and he moves, as it might seem, alone and independent, across his stage of history. But in the background was another figure. Wesley, like Augustine, had a remarkable mother. There are no long books about her, as there are about him. Here once more is an instance of the fact we have already noted: that most human histories have had only casual concern for the role of women. The activities of men, seen in events external and often dramatic and exciting, are abundantly chronicled; it is not so easy to chronicle the contributions of the women whose silent and subtle influence may have shaped the actors in the great events and made them the sort of persons that they were. The biographers of John Wesley give only incidental glimpses of his mother. But those glimpses are arresting. One looks at her, and then looks at the son; and begins to see that the flame that was in him may have come in large part from what burned at first in her.

Susanna Wesley, the wife of Samuel, the rector of Epworth Parish, was born Susanna Annesley. Her father, Samuel Annesley, had been one of the clergy who in the period of the revolt against Charles I and the royalist authority in church and state represented by the king and Archbishop Laud, had swung over to the parliamentarian and nonconformist cause. When the Commonwealth, which had been ruled by Oliver Cromwell and the Long Parliament, came to an end with the restoration of the Stuart monarchy under Charles II, Annesley refused to take the oath of homage, sacrificed his ecclesiastical living, and maintained his witness for presbyterianism and his protest against episcopal overlordship in the established church. His daughter, Susanna, inherited her father's strength of conviction, but also his independence of mind; and the result was that she arrived, when she was only thirteen, at conclusions opposite to her father's, and from that time on held to them with unshaken tenacity. Instead of nonconformity, she maintained that religion must have its strong framework of law and order. Whether she was right or wrong, the important fact was that when she believed anything she ordered her whole thought and conduct in accordance with it. She was to carry that sort of disciplined decisiveness into the Epworth rectory, and every child who grew up there was affected by it.

Two of those children were to become famous, John and Charles. Because the light of history has focused only on those, it may not be remembered how many others there were. Astonishing though it may seem by modern comparisons, there were nineteen. Once in about every twelve months there was a new baby. How they got clothed and fed and educated is still a matter for marveling; and it is not surprising that at one time Samuel Wesley went to prison for debt. He was by way of being a minor poet and a writer of not very consequential theological books, and he was faithful enough to his parish duties on behalf of what was often a surly and unresponsive flock; but the day-by-day business of making that crowded rectory into a home where the children could grow up into responsible men and women fell on Susanna.

When John Wesley, Susanna's son, was nearing the end of his life, he was still preaching fifteen times or more each week, and when he stopped in taverns at night he was "fully determined to lose no opportunity of awakening, instructing, or exhorting any whom we might meet within our journey." He had gone in his evangelical ministry not once but again and again through England and Scotland, from Kent and the coasts of Cornwall to the Scottish highlands, through Wales and Ireland, to London, Birmingham, Bristol, Liverpool, Dublin, and other great cities and villages past counting; and this was in eighteenth-century Britain, where railroads had not been dreamed of, and where John Wesley had to travel by stagecoach or in the saddle over roads that might be morasses of mud when heavy rains fell, or dangerous in winter from ice and drifted snow. It was estimated that he had ridden on his horse more than a quarter of a million miles; and the astonishing thing was that he said one day that he did not know when he had ever been tired. As an example of vital energy, it is no wonder that John Wesley has been acclaimed by admiring historians. But when all is said and done, was he any more remarkable in that respect than his mother? What he did was exciting, the dramatic movement of a public figure across a lighted stage. There was nothing so exciting in what went on behind the walls of the rectory set down in its corner of the Lincoln fens; nothing dramatic in nursery and kitchen and all the everlasting needs of nineteen children. But the mother who coped with that was the woman whose strength was reflected in her famous son. In this instance—as in many others—back of the person in whom a quality is most conspicuously exhibited may be the less remembered person from whom that quality came.

It might seem that when a woman had brought nineteen children into the world, and had had to see that they were fed and clothed and looked after day by day, she might have been so bogged down in sheer weariness that she would not have had much spirit left for anything beyond the plain routine. But with Susanna Wesley there was always the horizon of a never-forgotten purpose to which the life of her brood must be related. So far as her devotion could accomplish it, she would make it true that each child of hers—as the Catechism expressed it—should "learn two things: my duty towards God, and my duty

towards my neighbour." In a letter to John Wesley, when he
was grown and had gone to Oxford, she recounted what she
had striven to do. This is what she wrote—or at least a little
part of it; for the letter as John Wesley preserved it, and as it is
embodied in his Journal, fills more than five closely printed
pages:

July 24, 1732

DEAR SON,
According to your desire, I have collected the principal rules I observed in educating my family; which
I now send you as they occurred to my mind, and
you may (if you think they can be of any use to any)
dispose of them in what order you please.
The children were always put into a regular method
of living, in such things as they were capable of, from
their birth: as in dressing, undressing, changing their
linen, etc. The first quarter commonly passes in sleep.
After that they were, if possible, laid into their cradles
awake, and rocked to sleep, and so they were kept
rocking until it was time for them to awake. This was
done to bring them to a regular course of sleeping;
which at first was three hours in the morning and three
in the afternoon; afterwards two hours, till they needed
none at all.
When turned a year old (and some before) they
were taught to fear the rod, and to cry softly; by which
means they escaped abundance of correction they
might otherwise have had, and that most odious noise
of the crying of children was rarely heard in the house,
but the family usually lived in as much quietness as if
there had not been a child among them.
As soon as they were grown pretty strong, they
were confined to three meals a day. At dinner their
little table and chairs were set by ours . . . and they

were suffered to eat and drink . . . as much as they would; but not to call for anything. If they wanted aught, they used to whisper to the maid which attended them, who came and spake to me; and as soon as they could handle a knife and fork that were set to our table. They were never suffered to choose their meat, but always made eat such things as were provided for the family. . . .

At six, as soon as family prayers were over, they had their supper; at seven the maid washed them; and, beginning at the youngest, she undressed and got them all to bed by eight; at which time she left them in their several rooms awake—for there was no such thing allowed of in our house as sitting by a child till it fell asleep. . . .

In order to form the minds of children, the first thing to be done is to conquer their will, and bring them to an obedient temper. To inform the understanding is a work of time, and must with children proceed by slow degrees as they are able to bear it; but the subjecting the will is a thing that must be done at once, and the sooner the better. For, by neglecting timely correction, they will contract a stubbornness and obstinacy which is hardly ever after conquered, and never, without using such severity as would be as painful to me as to the child. In the esteem of the world they pass for kind and indulgent whom I call cruel parents, who permit their children to get habits which they know must be afterwards broken. Nay, some are so stupidly fond as in sport to teach their children to do things which in a while after they have severely beaten them for doing. Whenever a child is corrected, it must be conquered, and this will be no hard matter to do if it be not grown headstrong by too much indulgence. And when the will of a child is totally subdued, and it is brought to revere and stand in awe of the parents, then a great many childish follies and inadvertences may be passed by. Some should be overlooked and taken no notice of, and others mildly reproved; but no wilful transgression ought ever to be forgiven children without chastisement, less or more, as the nature and circumstances of the offence require. . . .

The children of this family were taught, as soon as they could speak, the Lord's Prayer, which they were made to say at rising and bed-time constantly; to which, as they grew bigger, were added a short prayer for their parents, and some collects; a short catechism, and some portions of Scripture, as their memories could bear. . . .

They were as soon taught to be still at family prayers, and to ask a blessing immediately after, which they used to do by signs, before they could kneel or speak.

They were quickly made to understand they might have nothing they cried for, and instructed to speak handsomely for what they wanted. They were not suffered to ask even the lowest servant for aught without saying, "Pray give me such a thing"; and the servant was chid if she ever let them omit that word. Taking God's name in vain, cursing and swearing, profaneness, obscenity, rude, ill-bred names, were never heard among them. . . .[3]

Parts of that letter will be read by exponents of modern pedagogy with a gasp of horrified amazement. It is obvious that Susanna Wesley had never heard of "progressive education," nor ever been instructed in child psychology. It is a far cry from her method of raising children to the present-day conviction widely held that a child must be encouraged above all else to self-expression and given freedom and opportunity to follow his own bent, without any rigid pressure that might thwart his inclination. And most especially, many would indignantly maintain that Susanna Wesley's principle of "subjecting the will" of a child was nothing less than barbarous.

Yet it would be fair to read her words with some interpretation. If subjecting the will meant to break a child's spirit and to render him incapable of positive thought and action, then she certainly did not bring that about in the case of her two best-known children, John and Charles. What she really wanted to check was not will but willfulness: the kind of fractious willfulness which a child left only to his own instincts, and without discipline, may intolerably develop. Moreover, she held to an assumption so instinctive that it never occurred to her that it could be questioned: that a child is essentially not an isolated and arbitrary individual, but a member of a family— and of a particular heritage—in relationship to which it will be his highest good that he should develop. She believed that there were old, proved ways of thought and behavior that bred strength and character, and she was determined that her children should not grow up untaught in these.

Now that the pendulum in contemporary emphasis has swung so far toward individualism, it may be well to consider the value in that earlier conviction. Self-expression may not amount to much unless the person is expressing a self enriched by something longer and deeper than his own brash impulse and ideas. As the pungent Dr. Jowett of Balliol once said, "We are none of us infallible; not even the youngest." And John Fiske, the historian and philosopher, wrote on what he called "the prolongation of human infancy," as a decisive factor in bringing the human race to what at its best it is. The young of most animals become mature in a year or two, or even in a few months, but with man there is the period of many years in which the child and the adolescent are still under tutelage and are absorbing the knowledge and experience of the long generations which have gone before.

It was by the establishment of definite and permanent family relationships [wrote John Fiske] that the step was taken which raised Man socially above the level of gregarious apehood. This great point was attained through [the] lengthening of the period of helpless childhood. . . . When childhood had come to extend over a period of ten or a dozen years—a period which would be doubled, or more than doubled, where several children were born in succession to the same parents—the relationships between father and mother, brethren and sisters, must have become firmly knit; and thus the family, the unit of human society, gradually came into existence. The rudimentary growth of moral sentiment must now have received a definite direction. . . . As the human family, with its definite relationships, came into being, there must necessarily have grown up between its various members reciprocal necessities of behaviour. The conduct of the individual could no longer be shaped with sole reference to his own selfish desires, but must be to a great extent subordinated to the general welfare of the family. And in judging of the character of his own conduct, the individual must now begin to refer it to some law of things outside of himself; and hence the germs of conscience and of the idea of duty.[4]

"Some law of things outside of himself . . . conscience . . . the idea of duty": those were the ruling principles Susanna Wesley accepted for herself and communicated to her children. Some things she was sure of, and that sureness gave her strength. When that sort of sureness fades, what once was the unifying power may give way to a troubled groping. In John Steinbeck's *Travels with Charley*, there is the account of a conversation Steinbeck had by the roadside with a New Hampshire farmer. What were people thinking about, there in his neighborhood: concerning November elections, concerning the world in general?

". . . People just won't put out an opinion . . ."

"Do you think people are scared to have an opinion?"

"Maybe some. But I know some that don't scare, and they don't say either."

"That's been my experience," I said. "But I don't know, really."

"I don't either. Maybe it's all part of the same thing . . ."

"Part of what same thing?"

"Well, you take my grandfather and his father. . . . They knew some things they were sure about. . . . But now—. . . Nobody knows. . . . We've got nothing to go on—got no way to think about things."[5]

Susanna Wesley did have something to go on. In a letter to her husband in 1712, when he was in London for a Church Convocation, she wrote: "As I am a woman, so I am also mistress of a large family . . . [and] I cannot but look upon every soul you leave under my care as a talent committed to me under a trust by the great Lord of all the families both of heaven and earth."[6] At that time there were eight children still under the rectory roof and old enough to understand; and so she would give one evening Monday through Saturday to each child—and Sunday evening to two—to read and talk to each one, and meanwhile "pray more for them . . . with more warmth of affection."[7] In her schedule for the week, there was "Thursday for Jacky." And in 1732, when "Jacky" had grown up to be John Wesley, Fellow in Lincoln College, Oxford, he wrote to his mother one of the long letters in which he told her what he had been reading, what he had been thinking, and what some of his religious wrestlings were; and he said: "If you can spare me only that little part of Thursday evening [which she used to give him as a child] I doubt not but it would be as useful now for correcting my heart as it was then for forming my judgement."[8]

In her essential qualities Susanna Wesley would have been notable in any time. But also she was a woman of the eighteenth century, not of the twentieth; and she becomes the more vivid when one perceives the conflict that was in her between her independence of spirit and the convictions of a century in which there was supposed to be meek submissiveness on the part of a woman and a wife. For the most part she spoke and behaved according to the pattern of the time, but there was always a point beyond which the integrity of her conviction could not be pushed around. The Rev. Samuel Wesley, her husband, was much annoyed when at family prayers he prayed for the new sovereigns, William and Mary, and discovered that his wife, who clung to the Stuart cause, refused to say "Amen." At another time, when he was away from home, some of the neighbors and parishioners asked to be allowed to come to the rectory on Sunday evenings to hear Susanna read to them from the Bible and other religious books. With the rigidity of mind which characterized most of the Church of England in the eighteenth century, and with which the evangelism of his son John was afterward to be confronted, the Rev. Samuel considered that his wife's action—the leading of a religious service by a lay person, and by a woman at that—was highly irregular and improper. But she was not easily overruled. She wrote to him: "I cannot conceive why any should reflect upon you because your wife endeavours to draw people to church, and to restrain them from profaning the Lord's Day, by reading to them, and other persuasions. For my part I value no censure upon this account. I have long since shook hands with the world. And I heartily wish I had never given them more reason to speak against me.

"As to looking particular, I grant it does. And so does almost anything that is serious, or that may any way advance the glory of God or the salvation of souls."

So ran her spirited defense. Yet there was another side of her thinking still to be expressed. She had read from books and tried to interpret to her unlettered neighbors what she had been reading. But then what? "There is one thing about which I am much dissatisfied," she wrote further. "I doubt if it is proper for me to present the prayers of the people to God."

Perhaps only an ordained minister should do that. "Last Sunday I would fain have dismissed them before prayers; but they begged so earnestly to stay, I durst not deny them."[9]

Even so, she felt that perhaps she had ventured too far.

Thus Susanna Wesley, for all her vitality and her courage, was not primarily an innovator. Her essential loyalties reflected all that was best in religious conservatism. She would not have visions and Voices coming direct to her, like Joan of Arc; but she was sensitive to hear what was spoken by inherited piety and the long witness of the church. In matters of the spirit she did what people of two centuries ago might do by way of parallel in the houses where they lived: When there was no fire on the hearth, there were also no such things as matches with which to light one; so the housewife would go to the house of a neighbor where fire was already burning, ask for some red coals, and bring them home to blow into a blaze under her own fuel. This was what in her religion Susanna Wesley did; and in that great sense she also was one who transmitted the living flame.

V

Elizabeth Fry

At the middle of the seventeenth century in England there came into existence the Society of Friends, or the so-called Quakers. From the fervent religious experience of one man, George Fox (1624-91) the son of a weaver in Leicestershire, the Society had its rise; but what George Fox found for himself came as the answer to what many had been groping for. It seemed to them that in the churches—which George Fox contemptuously called "the steeple-houses"—there was little besides formalism and deadness, with no spiritual fire coming down from the heavenly world to which the steeples were supposed to point. The Quakers were seekers after something that would feed their souls. George Fox, at the climax of his own troubled seeking, had been laid hold upon by a conviction of the Inner Light—a Light that had become smothered and forgotten under the cramping shell of ecclesiastical institutions and conventional forms. "When all my hopes in all men were gone" he wrote in his Journal, "so that I had nothing outwardly to help me, nor could tell what to do, then, O then I heard a Voice which said, there is one, even Christ Jesus, that can speak to thy condition, and when I heard it, my heart did leap for joy." Let any man lift up his heart to that living Christ, and the spirit of Christ would come to him, said Fox, "without the help of any man." And in the words of Edward Burroughs, who was "convinced" by Fox in 1652,

In all things we found the Light which we were
inlightned withall. . . . to be alone and onelie sufficient
to bring to Life and eternal salvation. . . . And so we
ceased from the teachings of all men, and their words,
and their worships, and their Temples, and all their
baptismes and Churches. . . . and we met together often,
and waited upon the Lord in pure silence, from our
own words and all men's words, and hearkned to the
voice of the Lord, and felt his word in our hearts to
burn up and beat down all that was contrary to God,
and we obeyed the Light of Christ in us. . . . and took
up the Crosse to all earthly glories, Crowns and waies
and denied ourselves, our relations, and all that stood
in the way betwixt us and the Lord.[1]

Thus, appropriately, the first name by which those who
gathered round George Fox called themselves was "Children
of the Light," then "Friends in the Truth," and "Friends."
The nickname "Quaker" was first applied contemptuously
by a magistrate before whom in 1650 George Fox and some of
his followers were arraigned, and in whose court Fox cried out
that all those present ought to "tremble at the word of God";
and the label continued to be applied to the Friends as they
witnessed to their belief that when the power of the Spirit
came upon them it might be "with fear and trembling." By
the authorities of church and state they were looked upon
with the shocked revulsion which established interests will
generally express toward what is new and challenging. Every
man following his own "Inner Light" in worship and behavior!
What would happen to law and order and all proper customs
then? What but anarchy and chaos? So the magistrates of
England, answering that question in the only way that seemed
obvious to them, visited upon the Quakers relentless punish-
ments. George Fox, who had gone into "the steeple-house"
in Nottingham one Sunday in 1649 and stood up to contradict
the preacher, was carried off to prison. He was arrested the

next year for "blasphemy," and spent six months "in the common gaol and dungeon." Seven times after that he was jailed. Other Friends were dealt with still more cruelly. Before the end of the century, nearly five hundred Quakers died while being held in prisons.

Men and women who endured what the Friends endured were made of heroic stuff. They had an intensity of thought and purpose which nothing could diminish; and because they believed in their special revelation, they deliberately set themselves apart from the general world. Therefore they developed ways and customs which should be the marks of their unmistakable separateness: the "plain speech" of thee and thou; the dress devoid of any ostentation or ornament; the meeting house stripped of traditional forms of worship, where men and women were to wait in silence for the moving of the Spirit. And in their daily living, shaped like their meeting houses in bare simplicity, they must listen only for that inner voice which should "burn up and break down all that was contrary to God."

But with the Friends, as with every religious movement, the passing of time, and changing circumstance, could have a subtle influence. Always it is possible that response to rigorous demands, which at first is like a fire, may begin to flicker. To be a member of the Society might become a matter of inheritance, with the old all-out devotion no longer there. By the end of the eighteenth century, this had begun to be true in regard to a considerable number who still counted themselves as Friends.

Among these was the family of John Gurney, a wealthy citizen of the county of Norfolk, where the trade with Flanders in wool and the weaving of wool had long been one of the chief sources of wealth in England. At Earlham Hall, his ample estate near the city of Norwich, John Gurney brought up his bevy of twelve children, for the most part as a widower, for his wife had died when the youngest child was not two years old, and the eldest only sixteen. Gurney must have been not only a devoted but also a very understanding father, for the whole flock of children at Earlham Hall grew up in happy comradeship. At that period in England, it was the custom for young people to keep diaries, and the adolescents at Earlham Hall did keep them, with a naïve particularity so fresh that, reading what they wrote, it is as though one could still hear their chatter. The Gurneys as a family had been Friends for generations; but to the Gurney boys and girls the Quaker conformity was mostly confined to the Sunday time of meeting. George Fox's rigid separation from "the world" was little in their minds. Among the worldly interests and pursuits which had been specifically renounced by Friends were cards, dancing, music, and the theater; but at Earlham there was plenty of dancing and music, and when the girls went up to London, there was theater too. There had grown up a distinction between "plain Friends" and Friends of less rigidly prescribed appearance and behavior, and the plain Friends were not to the Earlham taste. Nor was Quaker "meeting" always to the Gurneys' taste either. The name of the meeting house, which reflected its location, could call out some disrespectful comments from the young. It was in Norwich, on Goats Lane. One of the girls, Louisa, wrote in her journal: "Sometimes I think I will make better use of my time at Goats, but when I get there I seldom think of anything else but when it will be over." And Richenda was still more violent: "I had a truly uncomfortable cloudy sort of meeting. It was a real bliss to hear the clock strike twelve. . . . I sometimes feel so extremely impatient for Meeting to break up that I cannot, if you would give me the world, sit still. Oh, how I long to get a broom and *bang* all the old Quakers who do look so triumphant and disagreeable."[2]

Nevertheless, underneath the youthful rebellion against this or that, there were the deep foundations of character which their inheritance as Friends had given to all the Gurneys. And one out of that family was to show an independent courage and a fearless dedication worthy of George Fox himself, and to write her name beneficently in the history of England.

Of the twelve children in the Earlham household, seven

were girls. Catherine, the eldest, had tried to take her mother's place, when "my father," as she wrote in her Journal, "placed me nominally at the head of the family."[3] The third daughter was Elizabeth—or Betsy, as her sisters called her. It might not have seemed at first that it was she who would become the most distinguished; for she was the delicate one, shy and sensitive, and sometimes depressed. It seemed to her that she was not as attractive as the others. One day she wrote in her Journal, "I must not mump when my sisters are liked and I am not."[4]

But when Betsy was feeling well, she could be as gay as anyone, and as fascinating too. "I must beware of being a flirt," she wrote in her secret book. "I hope I shall never be one, and yet I fear I am one now a little."[5] Sometimes she admitted to herself that what filled her mind most was "dress and such trifles."[6] At the same time there was the deep current of other desires which flowed underneath the surface of her days. And this current was to be given new strength by something that happened when she was seventeen.

There came to Norwich from America a Friend named William Savery, who had had a "concern" to come to England and bear his witness in the Quaker meetings there. On February 4, 1798, all the sisters went for the usual Sunday two hours at Goats. Savery was moved to speak at the Meeting for Worship. After that, Betsy went to Uncle Joseph Gurney's house where Savery was a dinner guest. Later she drove with him to a public meeting in the Gildencroft. The *Norfolk Chronicle* reported: "On Sunday evening last Mr. Savery, from America, commanded the attention of a very crowded and respectable audience . . . for above two hours." After listening at this meeting to Savery, Betsy drove home in the carriage with her sisters —as Richenda wrote in her journal—"Betsy sat in the middle and astonished us all by the feeling she showed. She wept most of the way home."[8] Her emotional girlhood was in a turmoil. In her own diary on that same Sunday she wrote, "At first I was frightened that a plain Quaker should have made so deep an impression on my feelings [but] what I felt was like a refreshing shower upon parch'd up earth."[9] How long, though, would the spiritual refreshment last? With delicious honesty she noted two days later, "I rode to town and had a very serious ride, but meeting some one and being star'd at with apparent admiration by some officers brought on vanity, and I rode home as full of the world as I had driven to town full of heaven."[10]

All the same, the sisters and John Gurney himself were apprehensive. What if Betsy began to be carried away by "enthusiasm"—an emotion which the eighteenth century held in horror. She ought to have a change. So John Gurney determined to take her up to London.

They did go to London, driving the two-day journey in Gurney's own silk-lined chaise, with relays of horses changed at the inns where they stopped on the way. In London they stayed at Cousin Barclay's handsome house, and for a month Betsy was in a whirl of dinners, dances, the theater, and opera. But—in London was also William Savery, and Betsy heard him again at Westminster Meeting. "May I never forget the impression William Savery has made on my mind," she recorded. "I thank God for having sent at least a glimmering of light through him into my heart. . . . May I never lose the little religion I now have."[11]

Back at Earlham again; then, late in the summer, John Gurney took all seven girls to Wales and the south of England. If he could have foreseen what would happen to the daughter he had tried to divert from "enthusiasm," he might not have gone. For, in Shropshire, Betsy came into touch with her cousin, Priscilla Gurney, and through her with Deborah Darby, a fervent witnessing Friend. Now the leading that had begun with William Savery turned for Betsy into certainty, "I know now what the mountain is I have to climb. *I am to be a quaker.*"[12]

What should she *do* then to show her new dedication? She would look about for some who needed help. It turned out that near Earlham there were plenty. In Norwich were children ill-nourished and wizened who worked in the factories all day.

Betsy got hold of one little boy and taught him Bible stories on Sunday evenings. Others begged to come with him, until there were more than fifty. And as she went to some of the places where they lived and saw the hunger and sickness that were there, she expressed in her Journal the girlish compassion which was as spontaneous a part of her as was her unconcerned spelling: "May I realy be able to lessen the sorrows of the afflicted."[13]

She looked at the abundance of her own life at Earlham Hall, and the feeling pressed upon her that all this was "nothing without a satisfied contience." Also her "contience" told her that she ought to be not only a Quaker, but a *plain* Quaker. She knew this would disturb her sisters and her father too, and her affection shrank from "making the others miserable and laying a restraint upon their pleasures."[14] Nevertheless, she went ahead on her own quiet way. She gave up music and dancing, and she changed from her fashionable clothes to the Quaker garb, the dress cut on the simple lines, the white kerchief folded across the shoulders, and the high white lawn cap.

Now into her life was to come a new factor, in the person of Joseph Fry. He was a Friend also, of a wealthy family of bankers in London. He had been a schoolmate of John Gurney's, Betsy's brother, and that was how he had first known the Gurney sisters. Betsy had taken no particular interest in him, but his determined mind was sure that he was in love with her. In a visit to Earlham in July 1799, he asked her to marry him. "I discouraged the affair," she wrote. In December he was back with his suit again. She refused him again, but this time there were words in her Journal which showed that she was wavering. "I was not at liberty to say what the future might produce. . . . at *this time* I am not inclined to marry anybody."[15] But though she had sent Joe Fry home this second time rebuffed, she could not get him out of her thought and imagination. She had found when they talked together that they had ideas in common, and the same kind of "contience." When he came again to Earlham, in May 1800, he pressed his suit once more, and he brought it to a conclusion in a remarkable manner. He gave Betsy a gold

watch on the evening of his arrival, with an ultimatum which
is reflected in her Journal of the next morning.

> *Fifth month, (May) twenty-sixth. 2nd Day morn-*
> *ing before breakfast.* I went down to breakfast—my
> heart was full. I could hardly keep from crying before
> them all. I was so oppressed with the weight of the sub-
> ject before me, natural inclination seemed to long to
> put the hour of decision afar off, but he gave me the
> watch last night with this engagement. If I gave it back
> to him by nine o'clock this morning, he *never more*
> would renew the affair. If I kept it after that hour he
> never would receive it back. I found inclination, rea-
> soning and imagination so fickle that I saw my best
> plan was to leave them all and in humility to try to do
> the will of God, who alone was able to carry me
> through. . . .
> I did not feel *at liberty to return the watch.* I cried
> *heartily. Joseph felt much for me.*[16]

She still was not sure how much she felt for Joseph. But she
had not returned the watch. And on the next page of her Journal
she wrote, "As we spent some very pleasant time together in the
afternoon and parted comfortably, I trust all things will in the
end work together for good."

Joseph had won, and on August 19, 1800, in the Goats
Meeting House, he and Betsy Fry took each other in marriage,
according to the Friends custom of a silent congregation before
which the two who were to be married sat also in silence, and
then rose and recited their vows each to the other. Betsy admitted in her Journal that she "wept a good part of the time,
and my beloved father seemed as much overcome as I was." But
at length "the elders appointed broke up the meeting by shaking hands, Friends stirred themselves, straightened their bonnets and picked up their hats; and Betsy, leaving this time on the
arm of her husband, led the procession out of the meetinghouse
into the warm August sunshine."[17]

Now Betsy Gurney of Earlham was Elizabeth Fry of London. Joseph Fry brought her to his handsomely appointed house in Mildred's Court, next to the warehouse stored with the teas, coffees, and spices which the Fry family imported from the Orient, both a little removed from the rumble and confusion of the London streets. Yet it was very different from the wide spaces of Earlham Hall, and the young bride had her moments of homesickness as she adjusted herself to her new responsibilities, with Fry relatives making themselves at home in the house and with a flood of Quakers likely to do the same. Mildred's Court was ominously close to the building where the Quarterly meetings were held, and then in May the overwhelming Yearly Meeting. Some of the Friends from all over England had been accustomed to think that at Mildred's Court the door must always be open, and they descended on Elizabeth at dinnertime forty or sixty strong. Nor was that all. As Janet Whitney in *Elizabeth Fry* has piquantly described it, when the dinner had been served—as it had to be—in two or three shifts, "those first through swarmed upstairs to 'take a lay.' Beds and floors disappeared under billows of resting Friends; every article of furniture was submerged in the tide of thrown-aside bonnets and shawls; snores and stuffiness and confusion filled the house."[18] It was a strenuous beginning of domesticity for Elizabeth; but she loved Joseph, and in August of 1801 their first baby was born. Others followed every year or two, until by 1809 there were six, and Elizabeth did not have much time for anything beyond the house and the children.

But in 1809, with the death of his father, Joseph Fry fell heir not only to a larger income, but also to the estate of Plashet, near Epping Forest, as beautiful and spacious as Earlham had been. Now Elizabeth was the lady of the manor, and all the families in the little cottages round about became her people—and more attractive than the somber Quakers who used to descend upon her at Mildred's Court. The Church of England vicar and his wife found in her a warm and generous associate in whatever they did for the sick and poor, and in the establishment of a school for seventy children. She was reaching out now, beyond the immediate duties in which she might have been absorbed, to those whose needs touched her quick compassion, just as in her girlhood she had reached out to gather round her, out of the back streets and alleys of Norwich, the bedraggled children whom her sisters called "Betsy's imps."

Now unforeseen occasion was to bring her in touch with needs more desperate than any she had known before. In 1812, a financial near-panic so jeopardized the Frys' banking house that Joseph, and Elizabeth with him, had to go back to Mildred's Court. A harsh and unwelcome necessity that seemed; but as a matter of fact it was to open the door through which Elizabeth Fry, who otherwise might have been long since forgotten, would go forward to greatness of service and to enduring fame.

In this winter when the Frys were obliged to be in London, there came to the city Stephen Grellet, a French aristocrat who had escaped from France at the time of the Revolution; had gone to America, where he came upon a copy of William Penn's *No Cross, No Crown;* and was so moved by that and by a meeting of the Friends to which he was taken, that it seemed to him "as if the Lord opened my outward ear and my heart."[19] By this "Divine visitation" he was given a concern to go and preach and minister wherever he felt himself to be sent. He was not confined, as some of the Quakers were, within the tight little circle of ingrown piety. Coming to England, he "felt deeply for the sufferings of a large portion of the laboring class . . . great numbers out of employment . . . general scarcity of bread." He wrote in his Journal that the sufferings of the poor, "not only those at large and in the various poor-houses but also the inmates of prisons"[20] rested heavily upon him. He preached at the meeting house to an astonishing assembly to which he had invited and actually gathered thieves and prostitutes and the general scum of London. Also he went to Newgate Prison. To Newgate—as to most other prisons of that time in England —might have been applied the bitter words of Matthew's Gospel (23:27), "like whited sepulchres, which indeed appear beautiful outward, but within are full of dead men's bones, and of all uncleanness." Newgate, in its appearance from the street, was one of the handsome buildings of London, designed by the architect George Dance as his masterpiece, with monumental walls unbroken by windows, ornamented by statues in deep niches. But on the other side there was abomination. A writer to the *London Chronicle* put the stark truth in one sentence: "Of all the seats of woe on this side of hell, few, I suppose, exceed or equal Newgate."[21] And the worst part of Newgate was the quadrangle where the women prisoners fought and clawed and screamed in drunken degradation.

"They occupied two long rooms," wrote Stephen Grellet, "where they slept in three tiers, some on the floor and two tiers of hammocks over one another. . . . When I first entered, the foulness of the air was almost insupportable; and everything that is base and depraved was so strongly depicted on the faces of the women who stood crowded before me with looks of effrontery, boldness and wantonness of expression, that for a while my soul was greatly dismayed."[22]

And upstairs, in the so-called infirmary, Stephen Grellet "found many very sick, lying on the bare floor or on some old straw, having very scanty covering over them, though it was quite cold; and there were several children born in the prison among them, almost naked."[23]

What Grellet did next was to go to his friend Elizabeth Fry. And what *she* did was to gather some of the young women Friends to make flannel clothes for the children and the women; and in that January of 1813 she carried them to Newgate and insisted to the astonished turnkeys that she be let in.

At the moment it might have seemed that this was only a passing incident. Shortly afterward, the Frys went back to Plashet; and it was actually four years before Elizabeth Fry visited Newgate again. By that time she had nine children, and a swarming household of servants and guests to look after. Then, once again, it was the stroke of what seemed only misfortune that was to be for her as the touch of a divine hand.

The Frys' bank crashed, and Joseph Fry had to part with Plashet and go back to Mildred's Court. Now Elizabeth Fry turned her thought again to Newgate. By that time several groups of men, some of them members of the House of Commons, had become disturbed about prison conditions, and were proposing some large ideas that had no immediate impact. Elizabeth Fry, on the other hand, with her woman's instinct for the personal and practical, saw something that could be *done*. She would go and visit the women prisoners herself, and start her next efforts in the light of what she found.

So in January 1817, she was back at Newgate. She would see the women and talk with them. At the gate of the women's quadrangle, the turnkeys shook their heads. They never went in among that wild mob unless there were two of them together. And this lady? "Tear off your things—scratch and claw you—that's what they'd do, ma'am."[24] And the watch she had on: they would snatch that first of all. But Elizabeth Fry, armed with a letter from the Governor of the prison, stood there in her Quaker calm and her serene authority. She was going in; she was going in exactly as she was, and she was going in alone.

The gate was opened and the prisoners surged about her as she passed through. If she had shown an instant's fear or hesitation, she might have been in mortal peril. But before her Quaker garb and her steady eyes the astonished women fell silent. Then Elizabeth Fry stooped down and picked up a dirty child. Something must be done for the children, she said. They could all begin with that.

She had found the straight way to their hearts. She was reaching out to the mother instinct which all their sordid misery had not destroyed. She would start a school there in Newgate, and it would depend on them. *They* would do it with her.

Because she treated these women as though they were of some account, she woke in them a glimmer of their long-lost self-respect. Into the black hatefulness of prison life there came a ray of hope. They found one of their number who could teach, a young woman who had some education but had been committed for stealing a watch. Then Elizabeth Fry went to the house of the Governor of Newgate, to confer with him and the sheriffs of London.

Of course it was very kind and well-meaning of her, they agreed. Very well-meaning, indeed. But she did not know Newgate. These felons in there were impossible. Nothing could be done with them. And as for a school: even if there were any sense in trying to start one, there was no space in the prison where any such thing could be.

Elizabeth Fry went back to Newgate and found a room. Out-maneuvered, the officials grudgingly gave in to her insistence. The school was started. Then the women hung about the doors, tearful with desire that they also might somehow be let in and taught. Was there anything that could be done for *them?*

Yes, there ought to be, Mrs. Fry decided. Here were women in the vicious idleness of the prison, hungry to learn: to learn to read, to learn to sew, to do *something* that would be decent employment.

Another fantastic idea, the officials thought. What could be expected in responsible interest among these dregs of London, many of whom had been thieves and prostitutes?

But Elizabeth Fry was not easily deterred. She organized a group of ten of her friends into the Ladies' Newgate Committee. They would take turns in going to the prison, get materials for the women to work with, teach them to make clothes for their children, and perhaps something they could sell. The officials did not think anything could be done? Well, let them come with her one day to Newgate. So she got them there, the Governor and the sheriffs, before the assembled "female felons." She read to the women a set of rules which she had drawn up after she had first talked over all these with them. They were to promise to give up drinking, foul language, and indecencies of other sorts. They were to divide into small groups, and each group to choose a monitor of their own. Ladies of the Committee would come each day at nine in the morning and at six in the evening for a Bible reading. In the morning, materials for the sewing or knitting would be given out, then the women were to go quietly to work under accounting of the monitors, and at evening what they had done was to be brought in. There was to be no compulsion, and no punishment for any woman who did not work. Simply she would lose her chance. Did they want to pledge themselves to try?

"Let there be a show of hands." Then every hand shot up.

So with the power of personal compassion and with a trust that woke in the women prisoners a possibility of a response which all their degradation had not destroyed, Elizabeth Fry's experiment began. The result was what her serene goodness had believed in—and what the tough-minded had thought incredible. Instead of "the hell-on-earth" of Newgate—harridans fighting, screaming, cursing—the visitor to Newgate would have seen little groups of women in clean aprons making clothes for children, and then later things that they were allowed to sell. After a short time, the Mayor of London, the sheriffs and several aldermen came to look at Newgate. They found—wrote Fowell Buxton, Mrs. Fry's brother-in-law, and himself a member of the House of Commons—"what without exaggeration, may be called a transformation. They saw no more an assemblage of abandoned and shameless creatures, half naked and half drunk," but instead, what appeared as "an industrious manufactory or a well-regulated family."[25] And in February 1818, the Grand Jury of the City of London expressed their thanks for what Mrs. Fry had done, and declared that if her principles could be followed everywhere, "it would be the means of converting a prison into a school of reform; and instead of sending criminals back into the world hardened in vice and depravity, they would be restored to it repentant, and probably become useful members of society."[26]

Nor was Elizabeth Fry content only with starting a plan and a program for a group of women *en masse*. Her sympathy went out to them as individuals, and she stood by them at the times of their most bitter need. Women who were condemned to be executed—and in the savage penal code of that time there were many—begged for Mrs. Fry, and she went to them, with the comfort of her presence and the steadying help of her religious faith. She became convinced that capital punishment was not only horrible but futile, and she would afterward bear witness against it. Others also might do that in Committee hearings at no emotional cost. But to her, executions were actualities which haunted her, and the sufferings of condemned women she took upon her own heart.

Meanwhile, the area of her clear-eyed concern was continually widening. One of the ways in which early nineteenth-century England thought it convenient to get rid of its criminals—in addition to the multitudes who were hanged—was to ship them overseas to convict colonies, and particularly to Australia. Every little while a batch of women prisoners, chained and impotent but resisting wildly, would be herded from Newgate to one of the dreaded convict ships, waiting at the London docks. Mrs. Fry could not prevent this barbarous business of penal transportation, but she acted instantly to overcome its worst cruelties. She prevailed upon the Governor of Newgate to let her be at the prison the night before women were sent off: to read to them, talk with them, quiet their fears. Then she insisted that the women be sent through the London streets not chained in open wagons, exposed to the jeers and insults of the mob, but in closed coaches, protected by Mrs. Fry and some of her friends. She went all the way with them to the convict ship, read and prayed with them on the deck, and saw to it that every woman outward bound should have a bag of her own with clothes and little comforts and conveniences that she might need. As she left the ship one of the women leaned over the rail and called, "Our prayers will follow you, and a convict's prayers will be heard."[27]

Elizabeth Fry's work had been so extraordinary that it commanded attention, like the sudden shining of a light. In 1818 she was asked to give evidence before a Committee on Prisons in the House of Commons, and then there came to her an avalanche of letters of inquiry, and appeals for counsel. She visited the prisons in Nottingham, Sheffield, Leeds, York, Durham, Liverpool, and many other English cities. She went to Scotland and Ireland, and five times to the Continent. She had made her world aware of evils which few had been concerned about before; and by her own redemptive mercy she had shown what could be done for the reform of prisons, and for the regeneration of prisoners whom the complacent and indifferent had shrugged off as hopeless.

Yet, as was truly said of her, she was no professional reformer. Nor was there anything in her that was unbalanced or fanatical. Through the years when she was becoming famous as the Angel of the Prisons, she was also the gentle mistress of a household, the wife and mother in whom a family centered.

Her greatness had in it, of course, that element of personal uniqueness which can make an individual stand out like a genius in the midst of an ordinary generation. Any number of other people could have learned what she learned about the human wretchedness at Newgate. There it was, to be seen by eyes which looked that way, and to be a concern for any who were sensitive. But for nearly everyone else Newgate was not only something not noticed, but something that would have seemed none of their business if they had noticed it. One woman *made* it her business because her heart was tender, and because when her sympathies were roused she turned emotion into determined action. How and why Elizabeth Fry could be what she was is hidden in that mystery which is always involved in the difference between human souls; but it is also wrapped up with her inheritance and her chosen loyalties. She represented at their best the Quaker obedience to the Inner Light and the indomitable Quaker readiness to follow where that Inner Light might lead.

Loyalty as a Quaker was not always easy. As the years went on, some of the Fry children grew impatient with the rigid Quaker ways. One of them married a Church of England clergyman, and others of them drifted away from meeting. Most crucially, Joseph Fry himself was rebuked because he would go to the houses of some of his "worldly" friends to hear music, and disowned by the Quaker fellowship because his bank had failed. Elizabeth kept her deep commitment to what she believed the great ideals of the Society to be, while at the same time her own thought reached out to a more loving tolerance. "Children should be deeply impressed," she wrote, "with the belief that the first and great object of their education is to follow Christ and indeed to be true Christians"; and not take as guide to this and that "because Friends do it."[28] "I am certainly a thorough Friend," she wrote again, ". . . but I want to see more fruit of the spirit in all things, more devotion of heart, more spirit of prayer, more real cultivation of mind, more enlargement of heart towards all, more tenderness towards delinquents, and above all more of the rest, peace and liberty of the children of God."[29]

"More enlargement of heart towards all." Certainly it was to this that she herself had attained. And it was because of this that there had come true the prophecy which Deborah Darby made when Elizabeth first determined to become a "thorough Quaker": the prophecy that her life would be "a light *to the blind,* speech to the *dumb, and feet to the lame."*[30]

❧ VI ❧

Florence Nightingale

England of the early nineteenth century is separated by so wide a difference from the England of today that only by a deliberate effort of imagination can the gulf be bridged. The immense dislocation of two world wars, and the growth of a new social conscience, has broken up the stratification of rank and privilege which used to be taken as a matter of course. The riches and power which formerly were in the hands of the few—great ducal estates in rural England, palatial establishments in London, vast inherited incomes—have dwindled and largely disappeared. But a century and a half ago England still seemed almost as close to feudalism as to the modern age. What was then the expanding British empire had made the little island the center of the world's wealth, and that wealth was held by an aristocracy which seldom questioned its right to possess it. The common people, complacently regarded as "the lower classes," were supposed to be thankful for the crumbs. Meanwhile, the privileged moved in a world of luxury which for many was shut off, as by silken curtains, from any concerned awareness of what went on among the poor.

William Edward Nightingale was one of those who lived in carefree opulence. By birth his name was Shore, but he took the name of his uncle when he fell heir to a large inheritance from him. As an undergraduate at Cambridge University, he had already an income of from seven to eight thousand pounds a year. When he married the brilliant and beautiful Fanny Smith, daughter of another rich man, they went for three years to Italy, and in Italy their two daughters were born. The second was named Florence, because she was born in Florence and because her mother loved that city which seemed to her the most delightful one in Europe.

In 1821, when Florence was one year old, the Nightingales returned to England, to build a new country house, Lea Hurst, in Derbyshire. But no sooner was it built than Fanny concluded that it was inadequate for the kind of entertaining she proposed to do; so they bought Embley Park, in Hampshire, on the borders of the New Forest, and lived in the two houses according to the times of the year in which one or the other was more pleasant, and in the social season went to London. William Edward Nightingale followed the comfortable and casual life of the country gentleman, shooting, fishing, riding to hounds; while his wife, through her personal charm and her lavish hospitality, gathered about her a coterie which included some of the distinguished names in English society and politics.

Meanwhile, Florence was growing up, beautiful, witty, and charming—but unhappy. Why should she be unhappy? That was what her father and mother and her elder sister, Parthenope, could not understand. Didn't she have everything a girl could ask for—beautiful houses to live in, servants to wait on her, Paris clothes, friends, suitors, and every delight that the English countryside and London too could offer? And life in the family —what was lacking in that? More and more interesting and important guests were being drawn to Embley Park by her mother. And with her father, who had taught her Greek and Latin and French and German and Italian as well as history and philosophy, there was special comradeship for her mind. He was full of information, and he had a warm and generous way of imparting what he knew. There was nothing stuffy about him. Although he belonged in the ranks of the privileged, he favored the Reform Bill of 1832 which was meant to give more representation to the people at large. "How I hate Tories, all Beer and Money,"[1] he wrote in one of his letters. He was good to the tenants on his land, and maintained a free school for their children at his own expense. Was all this not enough to make Florence Nightingale content?

But she was not content. Something in her rebelled against the smooth, luxurious life she led. What was it all amounting to? "I craved for some regular occupation, for something worth doing instead of frittering time away on useless trifles," she said.[2]

Then when she was nearly seventeen she had a sudden religious experience. "On February 7th, 1837, God spoke to me and called me to His service,"[3] she wrote in one of the private notes which she began to form the habit of scribbling down and keeping. What came to this girl of nineteenth-century England is as a mysterious echo of that which happened to the peasant girl of Domremy in medieval France. Joan of Arc said that God had called her, through her Voices and her visions of the Archangel Michael and of her special saints. Florence Nightingale was convinced that God had called her. The difference was that Joan believed she knew specifically what God had called her to do. Florence Nightingale was convinced only that God intended her for some life different from the one she was leading, but she was still in the dark as to what the new way might be.

Meanwhile, the opposite influence of family and environment continued the soft pressure that could blur the reality of her "call," and keep her in the accepted grooves. Her father and mother decided that Embley Park was still not spacious enough for all the entertaining they proposed to do. The house must be rebuilt, and while the work was being done they would all go to the Continent. Nightingale designed and had built an enormous carriage, transported it to Le Havre in France, and from there the whole family set out to drive through France to Italy, the great coach drawn superbly by six horses ridden by postilions. To Paris and then through the lovely Chateau country they went, through Chartres, to Nice, over the Cornice Drive, to Genoa, to Piave, to Florence; then to Geneva in Switzerland and to Paris again. In the endless excitement of the changing scenes, the fascination of Italian cities with music and opera and balls in ducal palaces, it was not strange that the young girl of seventeen, beautiful and attractive, was caught up in such a whirl of pleasures that larger thoughts were crowded out. When after eighteen months the Nightingales returned, in April 1839, to England and the new magnificence of Embley Park, Fanny Nightingale, the mother, planning to have her daughters presented at Court on the Queen's birthday in May, was full of busy satisfaction in her confidence that Florence was being launched now on a shining social career.

But with the return to England there flooded back upon Florence the turmoil of spirit which had begun two years before. God had meant her to make something new of her life, and she had not done it. Under the bright surface of her days ran the deep current of unrest. Everywhere she was sought after. Men fell in love with her. The glitter of society attracted her. But "all I do is done to win admiration," she wrote.[4] And that was not enough.

From this time on the inner conflict deepened. She must find somehow a purpose big enough to satisfy her consciousness that she had had a call from God. She began to realize increasingly the shocking difference between the circles in which she moved and the lot of the masses of the English people. That decade in England was to be known and remembered as the "hungry forties." "There had never been a period in British history when distress and crime had been so general. There had hardly ever been a period when food had been so dear, when wages had been so low, when poverty had been so widespread, and the condition of the lower orders so depraved and so hopeless. . . ."[5] In rural England many who had tilled little pieces of land and been part of a stable population had been dispossessed and displaced by the expansion of great estates. The Industrial Revolution and the rise of factories had driven them into the cities and towns, where men and women, and small children also, worked at sweated labor through a twelve-hour day and went back at night into the filthy and sodden slums. For many of the well-to-do all this was a separate world outside their consciousness, but not for Florence Nightingale. "My mind is absorbed with the idea of the sufferings of man, it besets me behind and before," she wrote. "All the people I see are eaten up with care or poverty or disease."[6]

In the summer of 1843, Miss Nightingale spent much of her time in the cottages of the poor when the family was staying at Lea Hurst, taking food and clothes and medicine where they were most needed. Now the long question as to what she wanted to do with her life began to find its positive answer in her mind. Dr. Samuel Gridley Howe of Boston, one of the pioneers in treatment of the blind, and Julia Ward Howe, his wife, were among the distinguished people whom Mrs. Nightingale had drawn to Embley as her guests. Florence asked him if she might talk with him alone. " 'Dr. Howe,' [she said] 'do you think it would be unsuitable and unbecoming for a young Englishwoman to devote herself to works of charity in hospitals and elsewhere as Catholic sisters do? Do you think it would be a dreadful thing?' . . . 'My dear Miss Florence,' [he answered] 'it would be unusual, and in England whatever is unusual is thought to be unsuitable, but I say to you "go forward," if you have a vocation for that way of life, act up to your inspiration and you will find there is never anything unbecoming or unladylike in doing your duty for the good of others.' "[7]

As she began to visit the sick and to try to nurse them, she realized that good intentions were not enough. She saw a woman die because the neighbors, in the pitiful ignorance of the poor, had done the wrong things instead of the right things when they came in to try to help. And how much did *she* know? Very little, she had to admit. What she must have, then, was training. And where could she get it except in a hospital where the neediest sick would be?

But the idea of her daughter working in a hospital threw Fanny Nightingale, the mother, into a paroxysm of shame and anger; and, considering what hospitals actually were in that mid-nineteenth century, it is no wonder that she was shocked. For the so-called hospitals, in that period when next to nothing was

known of sanitation, seemed to represent horror and degradation
more than healing. The patients dumped into them came from
the alleys and cellars where foul diseases—including cholera—
festered. They came in filthy, and they stayed filthy. The smell
in the wards was so vile as to make anyone unaccustomed to it
vomit. To add to the general degradation, there was drunken-
ness not only of patients but of nurses, from the cheap gin
smuggled in. And who were the nurses? Women mostly disreputable, some of them unabashed prostitutes. Was this what
Florence Nightingale of Embley Park would go out to cope
with?

In dedication and intense desire, yes, already; and in the actual
fulfillment of what was to be her extraordinary destiny, the regeneration of the whole realm of the nursing of the sick, through
an unexpected and dramatic opportunity, very soon.

She had reached the point of resolving at last the long, and
what almost became the tragic, inner conflict between her passionate impulse to give her life to generous service and the personal involvements and family loyalties which had held her back.
Two men, one after the other, had tried to persuade her
to marry. One of these was Henry Nicholson, brother of her
dearest friend Marianne, and Marianne was distressed and deeply
offended when Florence told her suitor No. The second was
the brilliant and attractive Richard Monckton Milnes, with
whose nature and interests Florence Nightingale had much in
common. She had called him "the man I adored," but in 1849
she turned away from his final urging and refused to marry him.
In her private notes, as though she were thinking aloud, she
wrote:

> I have an intellectual nature which requires satis-
> faction and that would find it in him. I have a passional
> nature which requires satisfaction and that would find
> it in him. I have a moral, and active nature which re-
> quires satisfaction and that would not find it in his
> life. . . . I could be satisfied to spend a life with him

combining our different powers in some great object. I could not satisfy this nature by spending a life with him in making society and arranging domestic things. . . . To be nailed to a continuation and exaggeration of my present life, without hope of another, would be intolerable to me. Voluntarily to put it out of my power ever to be able to seize the chance of forming for myself a true and rich life would seem to me like suicide.[8]

". . . spending a life . . . in making society and arranging domestic things": that was what Florence Nightingale's family also wanted her to be content with, and her reluctance to wound them made it take a long time to break free. But in 1850 she achieved what she had been eager for since the Chevalier Bunsen, the Prussian Ambassador to England, had put it into her mind four years before. She went to Kaiserswerth in Germany, where a young pastor, Theodore Fliedner, had established a refuge for discharged prisoners, an orphans' asylum, and—most important for Florence Nightingale—a hospital and a training school for nurses, who were also to be Deaconesses and to make their nursing a religious dedication. The hospital itself was crude, and in its uninformed lack of hygiene, even horrible. But there at Kaiserswerth "Miss Nightingale found 'a better life for women,' a scope for the exercise of morally active powers. And here, though the field was limited, was provided in some sort the training which alone could fit women for larger responsibilities elsewhere. Here was 'the service of man' organized as 'the service of God'; here was opportunity for the Dedicated Life."[9]

She knew now the road she must take if she were to be true to herself, but in the loneliness of her choice she reached out wistfully for the understanding her family had not given her—and in their conventions perhaps could never give. From Kaiserswerth she wrote to her mother: "I should be as happy here . . . as the day is long, if I could hope that I had your smile, your blessing, your sympathy upon it; without which I cannot be quite happy. My beloved people, I cannot bear to grieve you. Life and everything in it that charms you, you would sacrifice for me; but unknown to you is my thirst, unseen by you are waters which would save me. . . . Give me time, give me faith. Trust me, help me."[10]

But when Florence joined her mother and sister at Cologne, "they would hardly speak to me." Nevertheless, she had made her decision now. The ties with home were loosening. She nursed her Great-aunt Evans through her last illness, and after that her Grandmother through hers—coming back to England for this from Paris, where she had gone to try to enroll for study in the hospital of the Sisters of Charity in the Rue Oudinet. Then a Board of Lady Managers in London, headed by Lady Canning, sent her an invitation to become superintendent of the institution which could have got its name only in Victorian England—"The Institution for the Care of Sick Gentle-Women in Distressed Circumstances"!

There Florence went to be—as her class-conscious and embarrassed family considered it—"in service"; and there she began to show the executive ability and the commanding power which now for the first time she could fully exercise. She was "here, there, and everywhere, . . . managing the nurses, assisting at operations, checking waste in the coal-cellar or the larder. . . . What was afterwards to characterize her work in a larger field was already observed in Harley Street. It was the combination of masterful powers of organization with womanly gentleness and sympathy."[11] For a year she gave herself completely to her institution—plus cutting short what was supposed to have been a brief vacation to help the Middlesex Hospital receive and nurse patients from the slums of London where a cholera epidemic had broken out.

Then in 1854 her proved abilities were summoned to meet a new and vaster need. England and France, allied with Turkey against Russia, were launched into the Crimean War. It began in September with the Battle of the Alma, which was a British victory; but in its aftermath came disturbing news. The *London*

Times had sent a special correspondent, William Howard Russell, to the Crimea. "It is with surprise and anger," he wrote, "that the public will learn that no sufficient preparations have been made for the proper care of the wounded." Moreover, stupidity and neglect in high quarters had brought it about that the most elementary supplies were lacking: no bandages at the battlefront, often no medicines where they were needed most. "The worn-out pensioners who were brought as an ambulance corps are totally useless, and not only are surgeons not to be had, but there are no dressers or nurses to carry out the surgeon's directions, and to attend on the sick during the intervals between his visits." And in the so-called hospitals "the commonest appliances of a workhouse sick-ward are wanting, and the men must die through the medical staff of the British army having forgotten that old rags are necessary for the dressing of wounds."[12]

What the correspondent of the *London Times* reported to his paper was only part of the ghastly truth. As the autumn of 1854 moved toward the end of the year, the British army was bogged down in its entrenchments round Sebastopol, which it had not yet been able to capture. Between the entrenchments and the army's base at Balaclava the only serviceable road was under fire by the Russian guns and consequently all supplies for the British troops had to be brought up over one rough track. There were no wagons or pack animals. Balaclava, though it lay at the head of a sheltered lagoon which gave harborage to ships, was itself only a fishing village, utterly inadequate to be the funnel through which must go the desperately needed food, clothes, fuel, and ammunition for the army, even if this had been arriving with any dependability from England. The terrifying Russian winter descended upon the Crimea, first with rain and wind, then with blinding snow. Caught without shelter on the wind-swept heights, the British infantry burned every tree and bush they could lay hands on as well as roots dug out of the frozen ground. There were only a few blankets, sometimes no food but dried peas and raw salt meat. The sick and wounded and mutilated

who staggered down to Balaclava were loaded on the decks of
transports, many of them with fever, erysipelas, and gangrene,
carried down across the whole width of the Black Sea to the
coast of Asia opposite Constantinople, and if they were still alive
when they got there, they found—what?

Hospital care, supposedly. But when it became known what
kind of care—or lack of care—there was, indignation arose in
England. The British Cabinet realized that something new and
different needed to be done.

One of the Secretaries in the War Office was Sidney Herbert.
Both he and his wife knew Florence Nightingale and were her
warm friends. On October 15, 1854, Herbert wrote to her on
behalf of the War Office. None but male nurses had ever been
heard of in British military hospitals. But Herbert believed that
women nurses might be sent, and thus not only "an enormous
amount of good will be done" for the army immediately, but
also "a prejudice will have been broken through, and a prece-
dent established, which will multiply the good to all time."
"There is but one person in England that I know of," he wrote,
"who would be capable of organising and superintending such
a scheme. . . . My question simply is, Would you listen to the
request to go and superintend the whole thing? You would of
course have plenary authority over all the nurses, and I think I
could secure you the fullest assistance and co-operation from the
medical staff, . . . I know you will come to a wise decision. God
grant it may be in accordance with my hopes!"[13]

Florence Nightingale's decision was prompt. She would go
and do what the Cabinet, through Sidney Herbert, was asking.
She set about the difficult task of finding nurses, difficult because nurses of character and of adequate training simply did
not exist. She selected thirty-eight from among the women who
came to be interviewed, and on October 21, 1854, she and her
party left London for France, to take ship from Marseilles a
week later, bound for Scutari on the Asian shore across the Bos-
phorus from Constantinople.

There Miss Nightingale found herself face to face with what

was the appalling result of ignorance and inefficiency If there was next to no scientific knowledge then concerning sanitation, even the little that could have been known by plain common sense had been ignored. The building which was supposed to be the hospital at which Florence Nightingale and her nurses would serve was a former Turkish military barracks. Built on high ground commanding a magnificent view, the great square structure with towers at its four corners seemed outwardly impressive, but to go inside was to find nothing but dilapidation and filth. The floors were broken, the walls damp, the courtyard in the center of its quadrangle a sink of mud and refuse. Rats and vermin infested the whole place. There was no heat except from a few inadequate stoves, no lights except from candles stuck into empty beer bottles, no sheets except some rough canvas, no decent place for cooking, no operating room, for many of the patients no beds and nothing to lie on but flattened out bags of straw. Into this barracks were to be brought a flood of sick and wounded so excessive—more than twenty-four hundred at the most crowded time—that there was hardly room to walk down the corridors past the patients lying along the walls. It was not a matter of dealing only with battle casualties; the Barracks Hospital had to cope with dysentery, typhus, and cholera too, often with medicines in short supply, and with food that was sometimes hardly fit to eat.

Conditions such as these would have been bad enough if they had been inevitable; but the fact was that they were due to a negligence made possible by a callous unconcern. At that period the British army was in large part the privileged preserve of aristocracy and wealth. Commissions did not depend on proved efficiency; they could be bought, and were bought. The gulf between the officer class and the common soldier was so deep and so accepted that the men at the top had only a patronizing interest, or no interest at all, in reaching across it. Almost anything was regarded as good enough for the rank and file. The Duke of Wellington had referred to his army as "the scum of the earth enlisted for drink."[14] A doctor who served in the

Crimea testified afterward before a Parliamentary Commission that "no general officer has visited my hospital nor, to my knowledge, in any way interested himself about the sick."[15] Florence Nightingale was to find that Sidney Herbert had been a long way from the fact when he had written her that she would "secure the respect and consideration of everyone." There were men in various posts of command who scoffed at having any woman connected with the army, who made loud jokes about "the Bird" and wanted to know, "When will she go home?"—before her nonsense began to turn the army soft.

But Florence Nightingale was not a person easily turned aside. Her purpose was too devoted, and her mind too sure, for any opposition to be able to block the road ahead of her. To her great compassion for all suffering there was added a disciplined intelligence. When she knew what needed to be done, she did not yield either to sentimental emotion, on the one hand, or to discouragement, on the other. She was determined to work in clear collaboration with the medical authorities, even when they were unwelcoming. She would put the group of women who were the best she had been able to recruit in England as potential nurses under strict rule, and make what they did so significant that the value of women nurses should be established beyond all gainsaying. And all that she expected of them she would exemplify by what she did herself.

No matter how wretched conditions were, she could show the men who bore the brunt of them that someone cared—and understood how much there was to care about. In a letter sent to a surgeon whom she had known in London, on November 14, ten days after she had landed at Scutari, she wrote:

> On Thursday last we had 1715 sick and wounded in this hospital (among them 120 cholera patients) . . . when a message came to me to prepare for 510 wounded on our side of the hospital who were arriving from the dreadful affair the 5th of November from Balaklava. . . . We have had such a sea in the Bospho-

rus, and the Turks . . . carry in our Wounded so cruelly that they arrive in a state of Agony. One amputated Stump died 2 hours after we received him, one compound Fracture just as we were putting him into bed—in all, twenty-four cases died on the day of landing. The Dysentery Cases have died at the rate of one in two. . . . Then come the operations and a melancholy, not an encouraging List is this. They are all performed in the wards—no time to move them; one poor fellow, exhausted with haemorrhage, has his leg amputated as a last hope, and dies ten minutes after the Surgeon has left him. . . .

I am getting a screen now for the amputations, for when one poor fellow, who is to be amputated tomorrow, sees his comrade die to-day under the knife, it makes impression and diminishes his chance. But, anyway, among these exhausted Frames, the mortality of the operations is frightful. . . .

Yet in the midst of this appalling Horror (we are steeped up to our necks in blood) there is good, and I can truly say, like St. Peter, "It is good for us to be here"—though I doubt whether if St. Peter had been here, he would have said so.[16]

None of "this appalling horror" did she evade. Her devotion to what she had come to do made her share it all. With a physical endurance which astonished those who saw her, she spent sometimes twenty hours of the twenty-four in the wards. One of those who saw her wrote that she "had an utter disregard of contagion. I have known her to spend hours over men dying of cholera or fever. The more awful to every sense, any particular case, especially if it was that of a dying man, the more certainly might her slight form be seen bending over him, administering to his ease by every means in her power, and seldom quitting his side till death released him."[17]

Operations in the crude surroundings of the Barracks Hospital could be dreadful, and wounded and maimed men, fated to undergo one, would sometimes think that they would rather die, but there by their side stood Florence Nightingale, and looking at her they could endure. After she had dismissed the other nurses, she herself would tour the wards at night. "She was wonderful at cheering up anyone who was a bit low," said one of her patients. And another one wrote this about her in a letter home: "What a comfort it was to see her pass even. She would speak to one and nod and smile to as many more; but she could not do it to all, you know. We lay there by hundreds; but we could kiss her shadow as it fell and lay our heads on the pillow again, content."[18]

Letters such as these made the name of Florence Nightingale known to thousands of people, great and small, in England. Suddenly she had become a symbol of what could be most gallant and beautiful in the midst of the agonies of war. Her mother and sister, and others who had formerly thought that nursing was beneath the family dignity, were caught up now in the great wave of pride. For all classes and conditions, from the young Queen Victoria to the fathers and mothers of the common soldiers, from the circles of the aristocracy to the taverns in the villages and the back streets in the towns, one figure above all in what might otherwise have been the ugly Crimean story stood out as glamorous. Henry Wadsworth Longfellow put into words what was already groping for expression in the thought of England, when he wrote:

> Lo! in that hour of misery
> A lady with a lamp I see
> Pass through the glimmering gloom
> And flit from room to room
>
> And slow, as in a dream of bliss,
> The speechless sufferer turns to kiss
> Her shadow as it falls
> Upon the darkening walls.

But Florence Nightingale was not looking for praise or for any personal recognition. She was too deeply absorbed in what needed to be done. She could not rest only with bringing the touch of her immediate ministry to men there in the Barracks Hospital. It was necessary to change the condition of that hospital itself—and of all other places like it. The agonies she witnessed were in part the inevitable consequence of any war; but what men were enduring there before her eyes was in greater part not inevitable, but the result instead of stupidity and neglect. She must see—and then try to get inept officialdom to see and to correct—the causes which made the hospital, and—as it sometimes seemed—the whole medical system of the British army abominable.

After the long hours in the wards, she would spend much of the night writing voluminous reports and recommendations to Sidney Herbert. As a result of these and of other facts published in the *London Times*, a Royal Commission was appointed to inspect the hospitals at Scutari and the installations in the Crimea. At Scutari they found what Miss Nightingale already knew, that all the ground under the Barracks Hospital was a cesspool of broken sewer pipes, from which foul gases came up through open privies in the wards. They found also what she did not know: that part of the water supply came through a conduit past the rotting carcass of a dead horse. These facts Miss Nightingale had not been able to deal with singlehanded; but already she had carried through the changes that came within her powers. She had a fund which had been raised by the *London Times*, and she spent money of her own, when no supplies got past the endless red tape of what was supposed to be the purveyor's office. She got scrubbing brushes to clean the filthy floors, bed shirts for men who were brought in half naked or in their blood-stained uniforms, the kind of food desperately needed for men half dead from scurvy. "I am a kind of General Dealer," she wrote to Sidney Herbert in January 1855, "in socks, shirts, knives and forks, wooden spoons, tin baths, tables and forms, cabbages and carrots, operating tables, towels and soap, precipi-

tate for destroying lice, scissors, bedpans, and stump pillows."[19]
Back of all this activity that might have sounded so prosaic
there was the awful urgency of life-or-death human need.
"Through all that long dreadful winter," Miss Nightingale
wrote, "I saw the men come down . . . without other covering
than a dirty blanket and a pair of old regimental trousers . . .
living skeletons devoured by vermin, ulcerated, hopeless, speechless, dying like the Greeks as they wrapped their heads in their
blankets and spoke never a word."[20] Gradually her burning purpose and her indomitable energy brought about the changes
which she alone had seen as possible. In May 1855, she could
write to Sidney Herbert of "the first really satisfactory reception of sick." Two hundred men from a transport were received,
bathed, their hair cut and cleansed of lice. Their filthy clothes
and blankets were taken off. They were given clean hospital
gowns and put into clean beds and fed. The Barracks Hospital
had become no longer just the last stage in a long horror, but—
as it was meant to be—a place where men were brought back
from death to life.

In that same month Miss Nightingale could feel that conditions at Scutari were sufficiently in order for her to be absent
for a while on an inspection of the hospitals in the Crimea, and
she went by ship to Balaclava. But the fearful strain of the
winter had taken its toll. She fell ill with fever and delirium, and
a few weeks later was carried back on a stretcher to Scutari,
still so weak that she could not speak. Even in the few days in
the Crimea she had seen conditions in the hospitals which filled
her with concern. She could not rest until she should go back
again, and early in October she did return. Now, more than
ever, she encountered the stubborn stand-pattism of army func-
tionaries, and in some cases a vindictive jealousy. Some of the
doctors were so set in their hard acceptance of what had always
been that they could push away new ideas with a brutal unconcern. The chief medical officer in the Crimea had warned
his subordinates against the use of chloroform in operations.
"The smart use of the knife," he wrote, "is a powerful stimulant

and it is much better to hear a man bawl lustily than to see him sink silently into the grave."[21] This same officer, and others also, had personal rancour against Florence Nightingale because the reforms which she had advocated had made the government at home aware for the first time of their own ignorance and neglect. By every device in their power the officers tried to undermine her influence, block her recommendations, write false reports of what she said and did. All this for her own part she could endure, but what tormented her was the knowledge that the common soldiers of the British army were still being exposed to needless sufferings which it was her whole mission to prevent.

In the autumn of 1855 Sebastopol fell, and the fighting ended; but then came the ugly aftermath, of troops waiting to be sent home, sick men still in the disintegrating hospitals, demoralization spreading as discipline relaxed. Back at Scutari again, Miss Nightingale found that convalescents let out of the hospital came back in twenty-four hours dead drunk. She did her best to get rid of the vile shops which had sprung up nearby to furnish liquor. She opened a reading room to which the men could go, and a recreation hall and a coffee house. Finding that many of the men could not read or write, she asked to be allowed to get a schoolteacher. The military commandant, Lord William Paulet, flatly refused. "You are spoiling the brutes," he told her.[22] Here again was what she had encountered so often and which could keep her—as she once wrote—"in a state of chronic rage": the contemptuous disbelief among some of those in authority that the ordinary man was worth any interest on the part of his "superiors."

In the summer of 1856 Florence Nightingale turned her face home. In two years she had set in motion an influence so far reaching as to make her name famous for all time. She had lifted the conception of nursing by women from something cheap and vulgar to a noble ministry. And she had brought into the whole area of medical care, and especially the care of armies, standards of efficiency which had never been there before. Among the people of England who knew what she had done for the British soldiers, she was thought of with a gratitude approaching adoration. The nation waited to honor her. There were to be triumphal arches, great processions, bands of music, welcoming orations. But to her the very thought of all that was intolerable. In her sympathy with wounded and dying men she had been through hell, and she could never forget it. She was haunted by the consciousness that thousands who had died need not have died if there had been responsible care for them, instead of callousness and neglect. "I stand at the altar of the murdered men," she wrote, "and while I live I fight their cause."[23]

The government proposed that a warship be sent to bring her home. Refusing that, she slipped into England and into London before anyone knew that she was there. She took a train alone and unobserved to Lea Hurst where the family were staying; and the housekeeper, sitting by the window in her room, chanced first to see a figure in black walking up the drive—recognized her, screamed, and rushed out to meet her.

The part of Florence Nightingale's career that became a romantic legend, the "lady of the lamp" at Scutari, was finished; but immense chapters of continuing work were to follow. "While I live, I fight their cause," she had promised in regard to the British soldiers concerning whom her heart cried out, "I am a bad mother to come home and leave you in your Crimean graves."[24] She refused all personal tributes. She made no public appearances. But with the help of Sidney Herbert and others whom her passionate zeal enlisted, she set herself to bring such continuing pressure upon the government as would lead to a whole new era of sanitation and preventive medicine in barracks and in military hospitals. It took 481 pages of Sir Edward Cook's monumental biography to describe Florence Nightingale's immense achievement in the long post-Crimean years, including the establishment of a new college to prepare men for army medical service, the founding of the Florence Nightingale Training School for Nurses at St. Thomas' Hospital in London, drastic reorganization of government bureaus to the ineptitude of which the worst of the Crimean tragedy had been due, and new measures for public health which not only affected England, but which reached as far as the cities of the Continent and the villages of India.

When Miss Nightingale came back from Scutari, weary, ill, and, as it seemed, with her strength gone, it was believed that she had only a few years—perhaps only a few months—to live. As a matter of fact the intensity of her purpose was like a fire more potent than any weakness of her body, and she lived to be over ninety. "Live your life while you have it," she wrote. "Life is a splendid gift. . . . But to live your life you must discipline it. You must not fritter it away in 'fair purpose, erring act, inconstant will.' "[25] In the years after 1856, when in the first of them especially she spent whole days propped up in pillows on a couch, she showed the other aspect of her astonishing genius: not now the figure of the "lady with the lamp," the angel of immediate comfort whose passing shadow was kissed by the men who lay huddled on the barracks floor at Scutari, but as A. C. Gardiner called her in *Prophets, Priests and Kings,* "the lady with the brain—one of those rare personalities who reshape the contours of life"; for she saw "visions and dreamed dreams which . . . swayed governments and built for generations to come."[26]

In Westminster Abbey the kings and queens of England of many centuries are buried; and buried there in that shrine of a nation's highest honor are also great warriors, statesmen, poets, men of letters, who have been the shining lights in their several generations. When Florence Nightingale died, the Abbey offered burial there for her. But the will which she had left made plain that she would not have it so; and the only inscribed memorial of her is a line on the family tombstone at East Wellow in Hampshire: F. N. BORN 1820. DIED 1910.

So her body rests in the quiet English countryside, in a grave as inconspicuous as might have been the graves of the men to whom she ministered. But her name is enrolled forever among the great of England, and among the immortal women of the world.

❦ VII ❧

Jane Addams

It is a happy fact in regard to some of the women with whom this book has to do that we can know a good deal about the formative years of their childhood as well as about their adult life. Joan of Arc told in her own words of what she did and of what she experienced in her village of Domremy when she was twelve years old. The qualities that made Elizabeth Fry remarkable were foreshadowed in the naïvely revealing Journal which she began to keep when she was a little girl. And in the case of Jane Addams there is the retrospect to which her thought turns in the first chapter of her autobiography.[1] "On the theory that our genuine impulses may be connected with our childish experiences, that one's bent may be tracked back to that 'No-Man's Land' where character is formless but nevertheless settling into definite lines of future development, I begin this record with some impressions of my childhood."[2]

What were to be Jane Addams' "genuine impulses"? They were to be an identification with all human need and suffering, in a wide companionship which reached out beyond her own class and kind to include men and women of every origin and every condition, and that kind of sympathy was present already in the little girl growing up in Cedarville, Illinois, in the years shortly after the end of the War between the States.

John H. Addams, Jane's father, had been a friend of Abraham Lincoln's, and in his desk was a packet of letters from Lincoln addressed to "My dear Double-D'ed Addams." Jane's mother had died when Jane was two years old, and her father was the center of her devotion. She admired him completely, and therefore anyone whom he considered to be great was great also to her. Two figures in their different ways were thus her childhood heroes. Her father was the symbol of complete integrity. He had been a member of the Illinois Legislature in the period of the War of 1861-65, and in the time immediately following when commercial interests sought their ends through political corruption; but Jane Addams proudly remembered what was told her by one of her father's friends: that although there may have been many members of the Illinois Legislature who had never accepted a bribe, John H. Addams was the only one he had known to whom no man had ever dared to offer one. And if her father embodied for her the ideal of integrity, so the Great Emancipator who had been her father's friend made vivid for her the meaning of compassion. When she thought of him, she thought of one who had lifted the burdens of those who had borne the heaviest loads.

The recognition of high ideals may produce a pious sentiment, and stop at that. Many people recognize great qualities of character, and approve what the conspicuous servants of humanity have done, without being stirred to follow in their steps. But the grave little daughter of John H. Addams had a sense of personal responsibility such as only the brave spirits have. The deep levels of her nature broke through her subconsciousness and were expressed in a dream which she repeatedly had. She dreamed that everyone in the world was dead except herself, and that if life were to begin again and the world go on, someone must make a wheel—and now that someone could only be herself.

The village street remained as usual, the village blacksmith shop was "all there," even a glowing fire upon the forge and the anvil in its customary place near the door, but no human being was within sight. They had all gone around the edge of the hill to the village cemetery, and I alone remained alive in the deserted world. I always stood in the same spot in the blacksmith shop, darkly pondering as to how to begin, and never once did I know how, although I fully realized that the affairs of the world could not be resumed until at least one wheel should be made and something started. . . . The next morning would often find me, a delicate little girl of six, with the further disability of a curved spine, standing in the doorway of the village blacksmith shop, anxiously watching the burly, red-shirted figure at work. I would store my mind with such details of the process of making wheels as I could observe, and sometimes I plucked up courage to ask for more. "Do you always have to sizzle the iron in water?" I would ask, thinking how horrid it would be to do. "Sure!" the good-natured blacksmith would reply, "that makes the iron hard." I would sigh heavily and walk away, bearing my responsibility as best I could, and this of course I confided to no one, for there is something too mysterious in the burden of "the winds that come from the fields of sleep" to be communicated, although it is at the same time too heavy a burden to be borne alone.[3]

Another sudden conception that came to the little girl—not a dream this time—was when for the first time she saw the back streets of a neighboring town where her father owned a mill. She had supposed that all the town was represented by Main Street, where she was fascinated by the toy shop and the confectioner's. But back of the mill was the shabby district where she first caught sight of the kind of poverty that is close to squalor. "I remember launching at my father the pertinent inquiry why people lived in such horrid little houses, so close together, and that after receiving his explanation I declared with much firmness when I grew up I should, of course, have a large house, but it would not be built among the other large

houses, but right in the midst of horrid little houses like these."[4]
Uncannily prophetic that was of the house in which one day
she would choose to live in the midst of the Chicago slums, but
it was even more important as another instance of "that curious
sense of responsibility for carrying on the world's affairs which
little children often exhibit because 'the old man clogs our
earliest years.' "[5]

The sense of responsibility "which little children often
exhibit"—those were Jane Addams' words. Whether that is
"often" the case may be questionable; certainly in the little girl
growing up in Cedarville it was true to an extraordinary degree.
Underneath the glancing surface of thoughts and emotions
which might have seemed to make up the nature of a child
there flowed a deeper river: the unfathomed river of a primal
consciousness which was to make this particular child become
a channel for sympathies as profound and timeless as human
life itself. In the same autobiographical first chapter, "Earliest
Impressions," from which quotations already have been taken,
there is Jane Addams' recollection of the altar which she and
her closest friend built by a stream where they used to play. "I
remember rather vaguely the ceremonial performed upon this
altar one autumn day, when we brought as . . . tribute one out
of every hundred of the black walnuts which we had gathered,
and then poured over the whole a pitcher full of cider, fresh
from the cider mill on the barn floor. I think we had also
burned a favorite book or two upon this pyre of stones. The
entire affair carried on with such solemnity was probably the
result of one of those imperative impulses under whose compulsion children seek a ceremonial which shall express their identification with man's primitive life and their familar kinship with
the remotest past."[6]

When Jane was eight years old, her father married Mrs.
Haldeman, a widow with children, and for the next nine years
Jane and her stepbrother, George Haldeman, were inseparable
companions, and continued as such until they both went away
to college. Jane wanted to go east to Smith, but her father was

a trustee of nearby Rockford College, and wanted his daughter to go there, and so it was to Rockford that she went.

The college was one of the first institutions for the higher education of women in the Mississippi Valley, and was called "the Mount Holyoke of the West." The fervor of its pioneer spirit still pervaded its student body: a consciousness of the privations and sacrifices which had made the college possible, and an intensity of purpose to use to the full the opportunities which had been dearly bought. "We worked in those early years," wrote Jane Addams afterward, "as if we really believed the portentous statement from Aristotle which we found quoted in Boswell's Johnson and with which we illuminated the wall of the room occupied by our Chess Club; . . . that 'There is the same difference between the learned and the unlearned as there is between the living and the dead.' We were also too fond of quoting Carlyle to the effect, 'Tis not to taste sweet things, but to do noble and true things that the poorest son of Adam dimly longs.' "[7]

At Rockford, Jane Addams' studies included Latin, Greek, natural science, history and literature, mental and moral philosophy, and French. When the college managed to get itself admitted as the first woman's college to participate in the Illinois intercollegiate oratorical contest, Jane Addams was chosen as the Rockford representative. She did not win it—which was not surprising in view of the fact that one of the orators was the young William Jennings Bryan. All she got was fifth place, "exactly in the dreary middle"; and when she returned to Rockford, the excited girls, determined to be content with nothing less than victory, left her in no doubt of their dejected feeling that she had let the cause of women down. Nevertheless, she was to graduate as senior class president, editor of the college magazine, and valedictorian.

At Rockford there was a strong tradition of religious evangelism. One of Jane Addams' classmates married a missionary and founded a school in Japan; one became a medical missionary to Korea; one became a teacher of the blind, and another a librarian in a pioneer effort "to bring books to the people." Jane herself was approached by an earnest member of the faculty with the appeal that she volunteer for mission work in Turkey. But though in this respect she put herself out of step with most of Rockford, she held back from joining any church. Some years later she was baptized in the Presbyterian church in her own home town, because she had concluded that " 'sincerely to give up one's conceit or hope of being good in one's own right is the only door to the Universe's deeper reaches,' " and because "something persuasive within made me long for an outward symbol of fellowship, some bond of peace, some blessed spot where unity of spirit might claim right of way over all differences."[8] At Rockford, though, her essential integrity of mind and spirit set up its barrier against the community pressure to conform. Here again her inheritance from her father was part of her instinctive nature. He had come from Quaker ancestry, but he was not a member of any congregation. And once when she was a young girl and had asked him about a religious doctrine which she could not understand, he had told her that he did not understand it either, "that it was very important not to pretend to understand what you didn't understand, and that you must always be honest with yourself inside, whatever happened."[9]

When Jane Addams finished her four years at Rockford, the institution was still called a seminary, and was not a college entitled to award the A.B. degree. But she and one other student had determined to be qualified for a degree if and when Rockford became a recognized college: both of them took a course in higher mathematics and Jane prepared a graduation address in Greek. The next year, 1882, Rockford did achieve its college status, and at the Commencement that summer Jane Addams was awarded her degree.

But what was to come next? Two purposes were uppermost in her mind: to study medicine, and "to live with the poor." Then came shattering events. In the summer of 1881, after she had finished her course at Rockford, her father, on a trip away from home, was taken suddenly ill, and within less than two

days was dead. It was the greatest sorrow, his daughter wrote
to a friend, that could ever come to her.

In the following October, Jane Addams registered as a student at the Woman's Medical College of Philadelphia. She
passed her first-term work with credit; but her father's death
had been a heavy shock, the return of spinal trouble which she
had had as a child sent her to the hospital for an operation, and
through the next summer and the following winter she was
mostly an invalid. For more than a year she had to wear a steel
brace for her spine. With physical incapacity and depression
of spirits, her plan to continue medical training came to an end.
In 1883 she was advised to get away from the discouraging environment of the recent months, and with her stepmother and a
group of friends she went to Europe—to travel in the British
Isles, Holland, Germany, Austria, Italy, Greece, Switzerland,
and France for what was to extend to the long time of twenty-
one months. Her intellectual and aesthetic interests drank deep of
the history and art of the old world, and in cities such as Rome
she had what she called her days of enchantment. But underneath
there was a weary sense of frustration and emptiness which no
temporary excitement could cover up. She realized, as she wrote
afterward, that "the pursuit of cultivation would not in the end
bring either solace or relief." And what she felt about herself
broadened into a general conviction which would later determine
the whole witness of her life. It seemed to her "that the contemporary education of young women had developed too exclusively
the power of acquiring knowledge and of merely receiving impressions; that somewhere in the process of 'being educated'
they had lost that simple and almost automatic response to the
human appeal, that old healthful reaction resulting in activity
from the mere presence of suffering or of helplessness; that they
are so sheltered and pampered that they have no chance even
to make 'the great refusal.' "[10]

One particular event had stabbed deep into her awareness with
its bleak contrast between the bitter realities of life and the bland
remoteness of the privileged and untroubled. One evening in

London a city missionary had taken a group of tourists including herself on a midnight tour of the city's shabbiest streets. It was on a Saturday; and because the Sunday laws prohibited the sale of produce on Sundays, vegetables and fruit too far gone toward decay to be kept until Monday were auctioned off for what they would bring. On Mile End Road, from the top of a halted omnibus, she saw two masses of poorly dressed people clamoring around the carts of hucksters under the flare of gas lamps which half-lighted the dingy street. Men and women were bidding their ha'pennies for what the auctioneers held up and flung to the highest bidder contemptuously when no one in the ragged crowd could bid more. From the milling press one man suddenly detached himself. He had bought a cabbage; and the instant it fell into his hands he dropped to the curbstone, tore at the cabbage with his teeth, and wolfed it down, raw and dirty though it was.

The sight of that hungry crowd was branded into Jane Addams' memory: the huddling figures in shapeless clothing, the cast-off finery seen only in East London; the pale faces with the desperate cunning of bargain hunters who faced starvation if they could not buy. "Yet the final impression was not of ragged, tawdry clothing nor of pinched and sallow faces, but of myriads of hands, empty, pathetic, nerveless and workworn, showing white in the uncertain light of the street, and clutching forward for the food which was already unfit to eat. . . . For the following weeks I went about London almost furtively, afraid to look down narrow streets and alleys lest they disclose this hideous need and suffering."[11]

Back in the United States in 1885, Jane Addams spent most of the next two winters in Baltimore, listening to lectures in Johns Hopkins University, but still uncertain and depressed. Her stepbrother, George Haldeman, was there, and his mother—her stepmother—was assiduously trying to make a match between the two. But the old congeniality which had made them so devoted in their childhood days was gone. His academic interests seemed to her to be often sterile; and her social concern had not much appeal to him. In the summers she went back to the old home in Cedarville, but it seemed empty now to her without her father. It was at this time that her baptism in the Presbyterian church, already mentioned, took place; and it may have been her loneliness most of all that moved her to this decision.

> There was . . . growing within me an almost passionate devotion to the ideals of democracy, and when in all history had these ideals been so thrillingly expressed as when the faith of the fisherman and the slave had been boldly opposed to the accepted moral belief that the well-being of a privileged few might justly be built upon the ignorance and sacrifice of the many? Who was I, with my dreams of universal fellowship, that I did not identify myself with the institutional statement of this belief, as it stood in the little village in which I was born, and without which testimony in each remote hamlet of Christendom it would be so easy for the world to slip back into the doctrines of selection and aristocracy?[12]

So her sympathy and her impulse toward human service kept her from settling down into passivity, but neither did she see before her yet any clear purpose that would command her energies. She was like a ship riding uneasily at anchor, but with no compass to point its course if it should hoist its sails. More years of what seemed to her futility were to pass before her life was launched on what was to prove to be its great adventure.

In 1887 she went to Europe again, this time not with her stepmother but with her friend Sarah Anderson, to join another friend already in Europe, Ellen Starr. In Rome she was fascinated by the catacombs, and in what they revealed of the corporate devotion of the early Christians. She had seen in London the settlement where young men from the British universities had gone to live and work in the midst of the poverty and degradation of the Whitechapel slums. Now she made up her mind to break loose from "the snare of preparation"—the long evasion of thinking about this and that and doing nothing. One day in Madrid in 1888 she determined what she would do. She would rent a house in a city "where many primitive and actual needs are found, in which young women who had been given over too exclusively to study, might restore a balance of activity along traditional lines and learn of life from life itself; where they might try out some of the things they had been taught and put truth to 'the ultimate test of the conduct it dictates or inspires.' "[13]

Hesitantly she told Ellen Starr of her purpose; hesitantly because she thought it might sound only foolish. To her delight, Miss Starr listened to it with warm response. Not only did she discuss Jane Addams' plan with quick intelligence. She would share it with her.

Presently then they parted, Miss Starr to go to Italy for a time, Miss Addams to England to visit the settlement in London which would have most to teach her, Toynbee Hall. In January of 1889, she and Miss Starr met in Chicago, to search for a neighborhood where they might begin. They were not asking for money or for any other help except the interest of persons who might be drawn into association with what they would try to do. The small personal income which each of them possessed was their only financial foundation.

One thing they could be sure of: that in the Chicago of 1889 there was plenty of room for service by people who wanted to be of help to hard-pressed human beings. A half century earlier, not a single house stood on the land by Lake Michigan where Chicago was to rise; there was only the unbroken shoreline and the empty prairies stretching to the west. Then with the great migration of the middle nineteenth century, the pioneer trains of covered wagons had begun to move, to be followed by the railroads; and tens of thousands of adventurous folk flocked in to what was to become one of the great crossroads of the continent. In the last half of the century, immigrants from Europe, looking for what they imagined to be the El Dorado of opportunity in the new world, filled the steerage of the transatlantic ships, and pouring by the millions into and then beyond New York, they turned what had been villages into teeming cities overnight.

In the nineteenth ward of Chicago—the ward with which Jane Addams would presently have to do—there were Irish, French, Canadians, Bohemians, Italians, Germans, Polish and Russian Jews, nearly all of them poor, ignorant of the ways of their new world, pushed about by corrupt and callous business and political exploitation, bewildered and unhappy. The houses into which they were crowded were dilapidated and dirty, with no decent sanitation, the streets unpaved and dimly lighted, and so foul that on one occasion Jane Addams found a foot and a half of refuse covering part of a block. Typhoid fever and other diseases had their constant breeding places in the filthy tenements. Gambling, drink, and prostitution flourished. It was charged that of the sixty-eight aldermen who controlled Chicago, fifty-seven had part in rackets which traded on poverty and crime. Carl Sandburg could see a kind of wild poetry in the brawling city. "Hog Butcher for the world," wicked, crooked, brutal, "fierce as a dog with tongue lapping for action," and "laughing even as an ignorant fighter laughs."[14] But there was not much laughter for the submerged people who felt the cruel pressure of the city which Lincoln Steffens could describe as "first in violence, deepest in dirt, loud, lawless, unlovely, ill-smelling, new . . . criminally wide open, commercially broken, socially thoughtless and raw."[15] It was this Chicago that would be the environment in which Jane Addams from 1889 until her death would live and work.

The choice of a spot at which to begin came partly by search and partly by happy accident. With the advice of some of the experienced residents of Chicago, officials of the schools, newspaper reporters, and city missionaries, she determined upon the general neighborhood where Halsted Street, one of the great thoroughfares of the city, was crossed by Polk Street, which ran

between the stockyards and the ship-building yards on the
Chicago River. Then one day as she was driving about she saw
a fine old house, set well back from the street, which survived
as a dignified relic from an earlier era before the flood of immi-
gration had poured in. It had been built in 1856 as the home
of Charles J. Hull, one of Chicago's pioneers. Battered by time
and changing use, turned into a factory and a secondhand furniture store, it was still fundamentally sound, and its large rooms
could be brought back to the graciousness which had belonged
to them when they were built and lived in first—before it was
flanked, as it had come to be, by a saloon on one side and an
undertaker's establishment on the other; or, as a Chicago wit
expressed it, by death and the devil. It was discovered that the
owner of this property was Miss Helen Culver, and through
her generosity Miss Addams and Miss Starr were given free
lease-hold of the fine old house, and they brought into it their
own best furniture in order that the house which they called
again by the name of Hull might bring to the tenement neighbors "all those adjuncts which the cultivated man regards as
good and suggestive of the best life of the past."[16]

When Hull House was established, only one other settlement
house—that one in New York—had preceded it. Twenty years
later, four hundred settlements were spread through the United
States. What happened at Hull House gave much of the inspiration which stimulated that development.

"To learn of life from life itself": that was one memorable
phrase in Jane Addams' first formulation of the purpose which
she held before her. She did not come with condescension, like
some superior being setting out to deal kindly with inferiors.
She came to associate herself with the everlasting realities which
underlie all differences of class and condition: with the hopes
and disappointments, the joys and sorrows, the quenchless as-
pirations and the never-ending struggle, of humanity itself. She
had the instant compassion for the poor which she had felt so
poignantly that Saturday midnight when she saw the desperate
hands clutching for the half-spoiled food on the Mile End Road

in London. The pathos of the sort of need which had been there
was present also in the teeming Chicago slums. Miss Addams and
the volunteers who gathered round her at Hull House did not
shrink from any kind of needed helpfulness. One time it was to
answer the frantic appeals of a lone old woman who was about
to be physically torn away from her few last pitiful possessions
and carried off to the poorhouse. Another time it was to take in
to Hull House for shelter a baby so disfigured and forlorn that
its own mother would not care for it; or again, a little Italian
bride of fifteen who had fled from her husband who beat her
every night when she returned from work because she had lost
her wedding ring. From the first, the neighborhood began to
know that there was no human service too lowly to be accepted
by these women who had come to live by their side, whether to
wash a newborn baby, prepare the dead for burial, nurse the sick,
or "mind the children."

But it would be a mistake to suppose that Hull House was
there only to mitigate suffering and to deal with what was
always squalid. Jane Addams and those who caught her spirit
did not look upon the men and women and children in the ugly
nineteenth ward as people merely to be pitied. On the contrary,
there was lively respect for the potentialities of all these folk
from many nations who had come to find America. In their old
lands and in their old life there had been much that was beautiful and distinctive: in costume, in music, in the sustaining dignity of ancient customs. The possible tragedy was that all this
rich diversity might be lost, and the human brightness smothered
under the leaden pressure of exploitation, poverty, and disillusionment. Therefore Hull House was to be more than just a
place for emergency assistance. Beyond that, and more important, it should be like a trellis on which all that was upreach-
ing in the nature of the immigrant citizens might climb and
grow and flower, instead of withering and being forgotten.
"Man doth not live by bread alone." These multitudes who had
had the virile courage to uproot themselves and cross the seas to
what they believed would be their land of hope had minds and

souls, as well as bodies, and Hull House proposed to feed them.
Always there was to be a sensitive perception of what the most urgent desires were, and a flexibility in meeting these. One of the early ventures which it would have seemed would be most important was a kitchen in which the immigrant housewives were to be taught the kind of foods that were most economical and nutritious. But as a matter of fact, that met with only limited response. Some of the carefully prepared model soups and stews were ordered in factories and imitated in a few households; but many were content with the idea which one woman expressed when she said that she didn't like to eat just what was "nutritious" but she did like to eat "what she'd rather." As a contrast to the kitchen experiment was the response to something so simple that few would have supposed it could prove remarkable. In the earliest days of the house Ellen Starr began to read aloud George Eliot's *Romola* to a group of young women, who listened to it entranced, and after helping to wash the supper dishes stayed to look at pictures of Florence and thus to have doors of imagination opened for them into history. Another memory, as Miss Addams recalled it, was "that of the young girl who organized our first really successful club of boys, holding their fascinated interest by the old chivalric tales, set forth so dramatically and vividly that checkers and jackstraws were abandoned by all the other clubs on Boys' Day, that their members might form a listening fringe to 'The Young Heroes.' "[17]

Yet to mention thus two or three of the specific activities at Hull House could be as inadequate to the whole shifting fact as would be one turn of a kaleidoscope. A kindergarten for the children of working mothers, a gymnasium for boys who would otherwise have been on the street, a coffee room to which men and women from the stores and shops and the public schools could come at lunch time, an assembly hall which could be used by the neighborhood immigrant families for christenings or weddings instead of having to hire a hall connected with a saloon, which had been their only recourse before—these were some of the more obvious developments of the settlement. But they were only the beginning of its response to the neighborhood, as the living impulses of its people—social, artistic, intellectual—reached hungrily for expression: response which included an art gallery, an exciting exhibition room which revealed the crafts and skills that the foreign-born possessed, a "Working People's Social Science Club," whose growing membership gathered every Wednesday night to argue and debate concerning the conditions of the city and their own life in it. So the settlement was becoming "a house of hospitality and compassion, of eager study and flaming indignation, where Christian love stepped out of the rarefied air of St. Paul's great epistle and met the common needs of Halsted Street."[18]

All these activities created for numberless people of all ages spots of new brightness in what had been the drab existence of the nineteenth ward. But for fundamental changes in their condition there had to be set in motion wider influences than programs carried on inside the settlement walls. Something had to happen to the whole life of Chicago, and to the entrenched forces that controlled it. People who lived in rotten tenements could be thankful for an hour they spent in Hull House, but that did not change the fact that the tenements were fire-traps and that rats multiplied in the filthy streets and alleys where the garbage lay uncollected because the city carts did not come round. Boys could listen to "The Young Heroes" stories, but the pool room and the saloon were still open across the street, and prostitutes were around the corner. Young girls might learn much at the settlement about how to keep in health, but that did not do them much good when they came home dog-tired every morning from working in factories all night.

What Hull House had to do was to try to wake a social conscience, and to get it translated into legislative action. Among the early residents was Mrs. Florence Kelley, strong, courageous, indefatigable. She inspired and organized an investigation of the sweatshop system, by which the clothing manufacturers turned over the bundles of unfinished garments to the women of the tenements to be finished at near starvation wages. Thus the employers saved the cost of furnishing decent quarters where the work might be carried on, and shuffled off responsibility for the human exploitation that was involved: the sort of exploitation represented by a little girl of four who was found pulling out basting threads hour after hour, "sitting on a stool at the feet of her Bohemian mother, a little bunch of human misery."[19] Nor did the evil of the sweatshops stop with the workers. Country doctors testified concerning outbreaks of scarlet fever in rural neighborhoods after the children had begun to wear the overcoats and cloaks which had come from some tenement room where the hard-driven mother had to sew the cloth next to the bed of her child who already had the fever. Mrs. Kelley's exposure resulted in the first factory legislation adopted in Illinois, setting up some sanitary standards for manufacture, limiting the hours in which women could be worked at night, and fixing fourteen years as the minimum age at which a child could be employed.

Laws such as these have now become accepted facts in most civilized communities, but for a long time they were bitterly fought. Within a year some of the protective laws enacted by the Illinois Legislature were ruled unconstitutional by the Illinois Supreme Court, and the struggle had to begin all over. The greatest service that Hull House rendered was in the willingness of its residents to come to grips with the ugly facts which the fastidious and timid looked away from as though they were not there. In Charles Rann Kennedy's memorable drama, *The Servant in the House*, the hero was the unregarded brother who turned up as the man sent to clear up the corruption from the burials underneath the ancient parish church. "By God, but I call myself summat," he dared to say. "I'm the drain-man, that's wot I am!"[20]

Jane Addams and those who worked with her were not afraid to be "the drain-men," to go where the muck and mire of the city's evil festered, to deal with what most citizens avoided as economic interests which ought not to be disturbed, and as "the

dirty business" of city politics. Miss Addams got herself appointed to the thankless job of garbage inspector for the ward,
with the duty of supervising the garbage collectors who were
tied in with city graft, insisting that the carts should come when
they were supposed to, and summoning defaulters into court.
Dr. Alice Hamilton brought pressure which helped weed out
of the Sanitary Bureau half its officials as ignorant or venal, and
so made possible clean milk instead of dirty milk for tenement
babies. She got new standards required for the midwives who
attended to the immigrant mothers, and she did what she could
to break up the peddling of narcotics. All these actions made
enemies for Hull House. Real estate interests tried to convey to
Miss Addams that money was available for the polite and proper
indoor proceedings of the settlement if she and her associates
would lay off the meddling business of stiffening the building
code. Others withheld their support from time to time when the
safe and privileged began to whisper that Hull House was too
"radical." But Jane Addams' conviction never wavered that "the
hoary abominations of society can only be done away by the
steady impinging of fact on fact, of interest on interest, of will
on will."[21]

What Hull House did for its neighbors was plain enough. The
work began with Jane Addams and Ellen Starr; within ten years
the number of residents had grown to twenty-five. At first all
the residents were women; later there was a nearby building
where men volunteers lived. All of them paid their own expenses;
most of them worked at their own employment for livelihood
through the day and helped in the neighborhood programs when
they were free. As the years went on, the total of those who
were thus identifying themselves with the neighborhood and
bringing to it their various abilities grew into the hundreds.
They did carry forward into actuality the purposes declared
in the Hull House charter: "To provide a center for a higher
civic and social life, . . . to investigate and improve the conditions
in the industrial district of Chicago."

It was not only the neighborhood that was benefited. Something else which from the beginning was close to Jane Addams' heart was happening. Men and women who might have moved only in conventional circles, and settled down at length into the bored dullness of their isolated privilege, were finding new dimensions for their living. They "did not come as reformers; they came simply as human beings, as eager to learn from their neighbours as they were to teach, and thereby create a fuller life for all."[22] Such a place and such an opportunity as Hull House represented meant—in Jane Addams' inspired imagination —not just a chance for a few conscientious people to carry out a plodding duty to "do good." Far more than that, it was their chance to find the wholeness of their own humanity. As she expressed it in an address which she gave at Plymouth, Massachusetts, in 1892, there is a "subjective necessity for social settlements." Too many young people in our prosperous modern America, she said, "have no recognized outlet for their active faculties. . . . Many of them dissipate their energies in so-called enjoyment. Others, not content with that, go on studying and go back to college for their second degrees; not that they are especially fond of study, but because they want something definite to do, and their powers have been trained in the direction of mental accumulation. Many are buried beneath this mental accumulation with lowered vitality and discontent."[23] But all the while, she said, there is an "impulse beating at the very source of our lives, urging us to aid in the race progress; . . . the desire for action, the wish to right wrong and alleviate suffering. . . . Our very organism holds memories and glimpses of that long life of our ancestors which still goes on among so many of our contemporaries. Nothing so deadens the sympathies and shrivels the power of enjoyment as the persistent keeping away from the great opportunities for helpfulness and a continual ignoring of the starvation struggle which makes up the life of at least half the race. To shut one's self away from that half of the race life is to shut one's self away from the most vital part of it; it is to live out but half the humanity to which we have been born heir and to use but half our faculties."[24] In other words,

Jane Addams was saying to all who had ears to hear: Float in the tranquil pool of a sequestered privilege if you are content with flabbiness; but if you want to have the joy of finding your full strength, then come to the side of those who are caught in the deep river of poverty and injustice, that by your help they shall not be swept downstream.

Thus far the woman who has been remembered is the one presented in the descriptive title of a recent book about her, *Jane Addams of Hull House*. It was there that the spirit of her life had its longest and most intense expression; there that, in the words of Walter Lippmann, she created "a citadel of compassion where the dispossessed and the bewildered, the friendless and the forgotten, have gone for refuge and refreshment and revival." But her sympathy and her constructive concern reached also to a wider field than Hull House, or the nineteenth ward, or all Chicago. In was all of human life, with its tragedy and yet its possible triumph, that woke response in her. As she felt the human oneness underneath all the racial differences of the old-world immigrants who struggled with the same conditions in the Chicago slums, so she felt "the solidarity of the human race," and believed that "without the advance and improvement of the whole, no man can hope for any lasting improvement in his own moral or material individual condition."[25]

No man, and no nation either. Consequently, when war came in 1914, Jane Addams was not swept away by the nationalistic emotions and the divisive passions which mastered the majority. With others who shared her convictions she founded the Women's Peace Party, which urged "continuous mediation" by representatives from the neutral nations, with the hope that they might offer proposals which would bring the struggle to an end. In 1915 she was chosen to preside at a Congress of Women from twenty nations, meeting at The Hague, which sent her and seven other delegates to call on the heads of governments in Europe with the women's plea for peace. These leaders received the women with politeness, and sometimes with more than that: with a sudden explosiveness of truth which recognized the insanity in which the world was caught. When Jane Addams began her audience with Prime Minister von Tisza in Bucharest, she said to him, " 'This perhaps seems to you very foolish, to have women going about in this way; but, after all, the world itself is so strange in this new war situation that our mission may be no more strange or foolish than the rest.' He brought his fist down on the table. 'Foolish?' he said, 'these are the first sensible words uttered in this room for ten months.' All that time the only clamor had been for more men, more money, more munitions for more killing. Now two women come and ask, 'Why not settle by means of negotiations?' They are the sensible ones."[26]

Nevertheless, the war kept on until much of Europe had been devastated. Then came the Congress of the victors at Versailles. Once more Jane Addams and women from many countries tried to bring a healing spirit to the peace which the men in power, the supposed statesmen of the nations, were about to impose. Meeting in Zurich, one hundred and thirty-seven women from twenty-one countries, both combatant and neutral, appealed first of all for a lifting of the blockade which had shut off food from Germany and the other defeated countries; "for granting credits to enemy and to liberated countries alike, to enable them to obtain food and raw materials sufficient to put them in a position where they can begin to help themselves"[27]; for a human compassion which, in Jane Addams' words, would be "the only thing, in this moment of sorrow and death and destruction, that will heal the world and bring it back into a normal condition."[28] Yet for eight months after the armistice the blockade was continued, reducing millions of people to near starvation, and creating the bitter sense of outrage and the festering hatred out of which Hitler and the Nazi savagery of vengeance would presently arise.

For her attempts to look beyond the particular passions of nations at war and to be concerned for human beings everywhere, Miss Addams paid a bitter price. When she had opposed the entrance of the United States into the armed conflict, all the ugly forces of suspicion and slander rose up against her. She had faced criticism and abuse before in Chicago, when sinister protected interests in business and politics resented the reforms she helped to carry through on behalf of the poor and the exploited. But the mass emotion which is roused in time of war can be even more merciless because it believes its passion is identical with patriotism. Miss Addams was spied upon and whispered against as though her resistance to war was treasonable. When the war had ended and she was still trying, through the Women's International League for Peace and Freedom, to make America understand that "the duties of family, nation and humanity are but concentric circles of one obligation,"[29] the D.A.R.—Daughters of the American Revolution—included her among the blacklisted individuals in its "Spiderweb Chart"; and members of the Ku Klux Klan waited with ugly menace at the railroad station in a western city at which she was expected to arrive. Even some of her friends deserted her; and it seemed in the sour decade of the 1920's, when America appeared to have no better purpose than "to get back to normalcy," that the generous ideals she had championed had become only a reason for contempt.

But in the long run the sun is more powerful than the clouds, and a great witness of the spirit, once kindled, cannot be permanently eclipsed. Before Miss Addams died in 1935, America—or the best part of it—had recognized again the nobility of her beliefs and the loftiness of her dedication. The country had begun to move at least in the direction of her realization that humanity is one, and that no part of mankind can achieve its destined life if another part of it is dragged down into the morass. In 1929 she was named by a widely circulated woman's magazine as the greatest American woman then living. In 1931 she was awarded a Nobel Peace Prize. And at a dinner in her honor in Chicago, Professor Charles E. Merriam of the University of Chicago said of her, "More than any other woman in America she has caught the brooding spirit of the mother and understood how to appeal to what Lincoln called the better angels of our nature."[30]

At the outbreak of the First World War, Sir Edward Grey, the British Secretary for Foreign Affairs, said as he looked out into the dusk of evening, "The lamps are going out all over Europe. They will not be lighted again in our time." As concerning any sure beacons toward a world of peace and happy promise, the lamps have not yet been relighted. They will not be lighted by nationalistic ambitions, by blind struggle for advantage, by more war. The only flame that can light them is that which Jane Addams embodied: an "active devotion to the vision of a world of peace, justice and friendliness, in which life not death is honoured, humanity not wealth is valued, love not hate prevails."[31]

~~ VIII ~~

Virginia Randolph and
Mary McLeod Bethune

It was only a short time ago that Negroes began to have the freedom and the opportunity to make their full contribution within Western civilization, and for a still shorter time have Negro women been able to do so. Yet already the names of many Negroes are written in the nineteenth- and twentieth-century records of distinguished service, and there have been others deserving of lasting honor whose names are not widely recognized because—and only because—the fields in which they worked were inconspicuous. In what they did and in what they were there was genuine distinction, even though for the most part, like the Unknown Soldier, they were "known only to God." Of such was Virginia Randolph.

Her life and work had to do with small schools in poor neighborhoods, where it did not seem likely that anyone could accomplish much of anything. But what Virginia Randolph did, though at first it might have appeared as no more important than the flicker of a single candle, as a matter of fact was like a flame passed on to many candles, so that in the end wide regions were lighted by it.

The War of 1861-65 had left the southern states of the United States of America impoverished. It was not until a generation later that economic recovery was much advanced. Even then development lagged in many important aspects of the

region's life. One of these was public education. School buildings
were mostly inferior, and the quality of teaching sometimes inferior also. At the turn of the century the schools were completely segregated, and the Negro schools got less support than
the white. Many of the buildings to which the Negro children
went, especially in the country districts, looked more like cheap
shanties than solid structures. Equipment was crude. There was
not much to make anyone want to be a teacher, or to interest a
Negro boy or girl in what that child was likely to be taught.

In 1892 Virginia Randolph, then eighteen years old, was
appointed to take charge of what was called the old Mountain
Road School, which stood on a roughly cleared piece of ground
on a hillside in Henrico County, Virginia. And who was Virginia Randolph? No one looking in at the shabby little schoolhouse where this Negro girl, then hardly grown to womanhood,
was supposed to teach, would have supposed that she would become significant. She was one of four children of her mother,
who had been a slave. When she was a small child her father
had died, and her mother had to make a living somehow for the
five. One room was all they had to live in. The mother got work
where she could in the daytime, and through much of every
night she was washing and ironing the clothes of white families.
There was a wood yard nearby, and the owner let the children
pick up scraps of wood to take to the one rented room that was
"home," and keep the fire going.

But something stronger than that fire of scraps was burning:
the flame of the gallant courage which the humblest human
beings, in the hardest circumstances, can sometimes show themselves to possess. This Negro mother had none of this world's
goods, but she had character; and she was determined that to the
utmost of the training she could give to them, and to the last
ounce of effort for them, she would make sure that her children
had character too. She sent them to school, with strict rules as to
when they must come back to her when school was finished.
And Virginia had no uncertainty as to where she was to be on
Sunday. "I was reared from birth in Second Baptist Church. My

mother would give us a buttered roll apiece, and send us to
Sunday School. We had to stay to morning service and had our
breakfast and dinner when we got back. Very often the dresses
we wore all the week were washed and ironed on Saturday to
wear to Sunday School. We often went bare-footed. Our dresses
were given by the white people and my mother taught us to
sew. She would cut them over and sometimes get two dresses out
of one."[1]

Martin Luther, in one of his indignant outbursts, wrote that
rich men's children too often "are complacent, arrogant, and
conceited, and think they need to learn nothing because they
have enough to live on, anyway. On the contrary, poor men's
sons must labor to lift themselves out of the dust and must endure greatly. And because they have nothing to boast about or
pride themselves upon, they trust God, control themselves, and
keep still. . . . Therefore, He gives them good heads that they
may study [and] become educated and intelligent."[2]

With his characteristic vehemence, Martin Luther was too
rough on the children of the rich, but he was right in regard
to the resourcefulness and strength that can belong to those who
have come from among the poor. Virginia Randolph was to
prove an example of that fact. She had never been accustomed
to much and so she could manage contentedly with little, and
use the little in such a way as to make more out of it. When she
had been appointed teacher of the Mountain Road School, and
found herself in charge of the old one-room ramshackle building on its red-clay hill and fourteen children who came from
Negro homes as bare and crude as the school itself, "having been
taught to make the best of what you have," she set to work "to
improve conditions."[3]

In the neighborhood accustomed to poverty and backward-
ness, nobody helped her at first; but until somebody did, she
would keep planning and hoping anyway. The woman who
lived opposite the school had a gravel pit, and Virginia Randolph
asked whether it would be possible to get some gravel to fill up
the gullies in the mud road outside the school. "Pay for the
hauling and you may have the gravel," was the answer. Virginia

had no money. But there were the children. So she organized a "Willing Workers Club," gave entertainments, and secured the necessary funds to haul the gravel. Next she managed to get some good earth spread on the hard clay of the schoolyard, and sowed grass seed, and then she persuaded some of the parents to bring young trees and plant them around the school—twelve of them, which "were named for the Twelve Disciples." Meanwhile she made the inside of the school look as cheerful as she could, with plants in the windows and a few bright bits of cloth made into curtains.

She began to visit the children's homes—if "homes" could be the word for the hovels some of them lived in. She found poverty, and often sickness made worse by ignorance and dirt and squalor. Particularly she came upon one woman ill with tuberculosis and with no decent bed or covering. If she tried to clean up that cabin she would be resented as officious. But there might be another way to help. In the school she began to show the children how to make dolls' beds out of boxes, sheets out of flour bags, blankets out of bits of flannel. The children were so proud of what she taught them to do that they all brought their parents to the school on "Patrons' Day," and through the children Virginia Randolph got over to the Negro fathers and mothers new ideas of what they might do themselves. Perhaps they, being her neighbors, could put together the things that Laurel, the sick woman, needed, and fix up the place where she lived. They did it; and the first step in Virginia Randolph's campaign for "better homes" had been taken.

As she not only taught the children cleanliness but kindled their imagination to see how, little by little, odds and ends could be used to brighten a barren place, what the children learned was carried home. The school affected the whole community. It was not only teaching a handful of small boys and girls some lessons out of books. It was spreading to whole families new ideas as to how they could help themselves.

It was not always easy going for the eighteen-year-old teacher; and she would need not only good intentions, but tact and quick-witted skillfulness in dealing with unpredictable people. The newcomer is always likely to be looked upon with some suspicion. Virginia Randolph set high standards for her children, and ignorant and lazy parents did not always like it. There was one woman who boasted that she "had whipped every teacher that had been at the school"; and when Virginia Randolph disciplined one of her children, she was set to repeat the performance. What happened is told in Virginia Randolph's own words:

> The children told me a lady was coming to the school, and by and by I saw a big woman standing on the porch with a long stick, taller than she. I was jus' praying, and was scared too. She said, "I want to speak to you," and I answered, "Walk right in. I'll speak to you in a few minutes. Wait till we have devotions." We got ready for prayers, and it happened that the verses that day were from the 13th Chapter of Corinthians. Then I said, "Children, this morning I'm going to pray, 'Lord, have mercy on dear mother that come to school; so glad to see you, dear mother.' " I was scared to death and without waiting I said, "Let us sing, 'I need thee every hour.' " When the children had finished I said to them, "Now, children, I know you all feel proud that this is the first mother that has been to school. She is a mother with two lovely children and you know 'the hand the rocks the cradle rules the world.' Children, don't you feel proud? I'm going to ask her to speak to us." The mother was touched, and with tears in her eyes she said, "I came for one thing and I have found another: I'll never come to disturb the school any more." She kept her word, and became one of the school's Willing Workers. Soon afterwards she had a picture made of me, and hung it on the walls of her house.[4]

"Thus," as was written by a tutor in the Oxford University Department of Education who had come to America to study the schools in the states of the South, "by incessant toil, great determination, and an unselfishness and singleness of purpose which disarmed her critics, this slightly built Negro woman rallied the school patrons around her, and made her little school a centre of light and life in the community. . . ."[5] Without neglecting the teaching of the usual school subjects, she gradually enlarged the range and scope of what had by this time come to be known as "industrial education." She believed firmly in "learning by doing," and in honest work as the best of all character builders. She went unassumingly to some of the white schools which were beginning to be given resources that she did not have, and begged from them leftover bits of dress material and reed and raffia, which she brought back to her colored children as she taught them to sew and weave.

The Superintendent of Schools for Henrico County was the alert and able Jackson Davis. He noticed what Virginia Randolph was doing, and his quick perception saw its wide significance. "Here was a teacher," he said, "who thought of her work in terms of the welfare of a whole community, and of the school as an agency to help people to live better, to do their work with more skill and intelligence, and to do it in the spirit of neighborliness."[6] What she was doing ought to be done at other places too. But how to bring that about?

His first idea was to have Miss Randolph visit rural schools in the county one or two days a week, to help the teachers there see what they could try, while a substitute took her place for those days at Mountain Road. But suppose he could manage to have her give her whole time to teaching teachers? That would be better still—if only he had the money to create a new position.

Meanwhile, a Quaker lady in Philadelphia, Miss Anna T. Jeanes, living in a Home for the Aged which she herself had created, had other property which she wanted to bequeath to a cause that would help those who needed it most. Hampton Institute, dedicated to the training, both academic and industrial, of Negro youth, had had its small beginning in 1861; and then, under the noble leadership of General Samuel C. Armstrong, who came to its leadership in 1866, had grown to be a great school. Miss Jeanes was thoroughly in sympathy with its work; but when Dr. Hollis B. Frissell, its principal, came to see her in 1904 to ask for help for Hampton she had other and particular ideas. She wanted to help "the poor little Negro cabin one-teacher rural schools." So Dr. Frissell helped her to formulate the endowment which was to be known thereafter as the Jeanes Fund, for "the one purpose of assisting in the Southern United States, Community, County, or Rural Schools for that great class of Negroes to whom the small rural and community schools are alone available."[7] The executive director of that fund was Dr. James Hardy Dillard, and to him Mr. Jackson Davis wrote an appeal for a grant which would enable him to make Miss Virginia Randolph a supervising teacher.

The grant was forthcoming. Incredible as it may seem—as representing, on the one hand, the greater relative value of a dollar a half century ago, and, on the other hand, the pitiful meagerness at best of teachers' salaries then—Virginia Randolph was to receive forty dollars a month. At Mr. Davis' persuasion, she gave up her school—though her devotion to this place to which she had given her whole heart was so great that she did not want to leave—and became the first Jeanes Teacher: the first in a great, increasing company who were to bring incalculable stimulus to the little Negro schools throughout the South. From 1908 for more than a quarter of a century she was supervisor of Negro schools in Henrico County. She saw the one-room school with its fourteen children, to which she had come at first, grow into its transformation as the Virginia Randolph County Training School, with an enrollment of 235 pupils, of whom 75 were in the high school grades. And she saw the example which she had set, in what had seemed her obscure and unimportant place, admired and studied by educators not only of her own country but of other countries in the world where there were disadvantaged people.

Under Dr. Dillard and his successors, the Jeanes Fund offered to pay the salaries of Jeanes Teachers in one after another of the southern states, as a new leaven in the whole area of Negro education. Then the state departments of public education, recognizing the great benefit which the Jeanes Teachers were bringing to the Negro schools, began to make provision in the official budgets for their continuance and for enlargement of their numbers. In 1908 Miss Randolph was the lone pioneer; forty years later the number of Jeanes Teachers in the South had grown to more than five hundred. The entire appropriation for Miss Randolph's salary the first year, coming from the Jeanes Fund, was $360.00. Forty years later the constantly increasing gifts of the Jeanes Fund to sponsor Jeanes Teachers in new areas, to a maximum subsidy in one year of $118,391.00 had so stimulated the responsible interest of the state boards of education that public annual appropriations for the Jeanes work had risen even then to one and one-quarter million dollars; and in 1963 it had come to pass that every state in the South, and practically every county, had its Jeanes Teachers supported entirely by public funds. What began as a tiny venture had grown into a great and indispensable fact.

When Virginia Randolph died in 1958 she could know that for all her life the words were true which Jackson Davis had spoken in the address he made at the dedication of the new school, bearing her name, at the old Mountain Road site. She had been "a leader by being a servant of all"; she had had "a genius for doing the simple little things that make up the larger things in education and in character"; and her work, which began in the poor little building on a side road of Henrico County, had become "a shining light."[8]

Mary McLeod Bethune

Of the same generation as Virginia Randolph was another woman who came up from even more harsh conditions, became more widely known, and reached achievements which showed how great can be the contributions which the Negro can make to American life.

Mary Jane McLeod was born in Mayesville, South Carolina,

in 1875. Her father and mother had both been slaves on neigh-boring plantations. When the War of 1861-65 had ended and the slaves were free, Samuel McLeod worked for his former master, and earned enough to buy thirty-five acres of land with a pineboard cabin on it. Besides the cabin and the land, about all he owned was a cow and a mule and a plow. Every year he planted his acres in cotton, and through the long hot summer the whole family spent most of its time grubbing out the crab grass from around the cotton plants and trying to make sure that there would be a crop in the fall which could be sold for enough to carry them through the winter. Nobody in the family had any education, and it did not seem likely that the chance for it would come. One disastrous year the tired old mule stopped in the middle of the plowing, fell down in the furrow, and died; and for the rest of that season the older children had to take turns trying to pull the plow. First and last, there were seventeen children in the four-room cabin, Mary Jane being the fourteenth. If Sam McLeod could get enough fatback and hominy grits to keep them fed, that was about the utmost he could manage, without any notion of children getting free from the cotton field to go to school.

But one child did want to go—if there had been in Mayesville such a thing as a school for a Negro child to go to. One day Mary Jane went with her mother who was carrying back the clothes she had washed for the white family to whom she had formerly belonged. Two little grandchildren of the family were in their playhouse out in the yard, and as Mary Jane went by they called her in to play nurse for their dolls. On a table was something she picked up to look at. "Put down that book," said one of the little white childen, "*You* can't read."[9] Hurt and ashamed, she put the book down. No, she could not read. But some day she was going to learn.

Out of the blue the chance came. One day there appeared in Mayesville a woman who called herself Miss Wilson. The Mission Board of the Presbyterian Church had sent her to start a school for Negro children, and she went from cabin to cabin to see what children might be allowed to come. "Yes," said Sam McLeod, now that cotton picking was over, "Mary Jane can go." With a little money he had, he took the excited girl to the Mayesville general store and bought her a slate with a piece of chalk tied to it by a string.

So Mary Jane—or Janie, as her teacher called her—went to school, five miles there and five miles back every day by the road she had to walk to the shack near the railroad in Mayesville, which was the best place Miss Wilson could find. By the second winter, there was a better building, two rooms, and built of brick. It was "Mayesville Institute" now, the only school for Negro children in the whole vicinity, and Janie stayed there through the elementary grades, which were all that the school could teach. Then back to the cabin, and to work in the cotton field again.

But what seemed like another miracle was to happen. One day when Mary Jane was in the cotton field, Miss Wilson appeared, walking fast. "I want to talk to you," she called. And what she had to say was this: A white lady in Denver, Colorado, had decided to use her life's savings to help some Negro child get more education, and Miss Wilson had chosen Mary Jane McLeod from those who had been to the Mayesville School as the one who should have the scholarship.

Soon afterward for the first time in her life she was on a railroad train, traveling to Concord, North Carolina. There she was enrolled in Scotia Seminary, which had been founded in 1867, where she was to spend seven years. The scholarship from the lady in Colorado had made possible her being there, but by itself it was not enough to cover her bare needs. She could not afford to go home in the summers, but worked through all her free weeks as cook, chambermaid, or as laundress with various white families. At one time in the school session she owned only one shirtwaist, which she had to wash in the evening to wear again the next day—until she found some clothes in one of the "missionary barrels" which had been sent to the school.

When she was ready to graduate from Scotia, she told the

president that she would like to be a missionary to Africa, and he advised her to try to be admitted to the Moody Bible Institute in Chicago. She did apply and was admitted; but before the fall term began she went back home again, for the first time since as a little girl of twelve she had climbed on the train that took her away from Mayesville. There was wonder and jubilation among the Negro neighbors. This girl who had grown up in the McLeod cabin was educated! She held classes three evenings a week for all who wanted to come, and she taught the children in the Sunday School. Perhaps she was part of a new emancipation, not out of slavery only, but out of ignorance and inferiority. There could be a new lift of emotion as Negro voices sang again the haunting spiritual, "Go down, Moses, go down Moses, tell old Pharaoh, let my people go!"

At the Moody Bible Institute, so Mary McLeod wrote afterward, "There were no feelings of race. . . . There we learned to look upon a man as a man, not as a Caucasian or a Negro. . . . under this benign influence, including that of Dwight L. Moody, a love for the whole human race, regardless of creed, class, or color, entered my soul and remains with me, thank God, to this day."[10] For "field work" at the Institute there was plenty to do, ministering to the poor and the sick, services at prisons, evangelistic efforts—sometimes not without danger—in the Chicago slums. When she graduated she went to New York to ask the Presbyterian Board of Missions for an appointment in Africa. "No," they answered. They had no position open then. All they could offer her was an assignment as a teacher at Haines Normal Institute in Augusta, Georgia.

At the moment, that was a cruel disappointment. To go to Africa had kindled her imagination, as something large and exciting. But to go to Georgia, to Georgia where the Ku Klux Klan was riding high, what could that mean except frustration for a Negro girl? But it was to Georgia that she went; and soon in Augusta she was putting all her vigor into work with the Negro children there, and after that for two years at another Negro school in Sumter.

The next thing that happened was that she met Albertus Bethune, who fell in love with her, and before long they were married. Now she dropped the "Jane" from what would be too long a name, to be thenceforth Mary McLeod Bethune. They moved to Savannah, where Albertus Bethune had an appointment as a teacher; and there a son was born. Later they went to Florida. She was possessed with a desire to start a school that she herself could shape, and into which she could pour her restless passion to be of service to Negro children who had to begin—as she had begun—with next to nothing. Albertus Bethune did not have her ambition, but he co-operated as well as he knew how. Presently they were in Daytona, Albertus driving a horse and buggy for hire, Mary trying to launch her school.

She had come to Daytona on the Jim Crow coach, and when she walked along the railroad station platform she knew that there was work here for someone to do. The Florida East Coast Railroad was being extended down the state. Negro laborers were building it, and along the Halifax River, Negroes were living in crowded hovels, with children spilling out into the streets and alleys.

On unpaved Oak Street she saw a house with four small rooms downstairs and three above that could be rented for eleven dollars a month. All she had was a dollar and a half, but the owner of the house let her have it on credit. She went to the town dump-heap and to the back doors of Daytona resort hotels to find any old and broken furniture that she could salvage; she picked up packing boxes here and there that might be turned into desks; she begged some other things she had to have—a broom, a lamp or two, a few old dishes. She made pies and sold them to the laborers along the railroad tracks to get some money; and on October 3, 1904, she opened the Daytona Educational and Industrial Training School for Negro Girls, with five girls ranging from eight to twelve, and one small boy, her own. The parents were to pay fifty cents a week for each child—if they had the money. "This is a new kind of school," Mary Bethune said. "I am going to teach my girls crafts and home-making. I am going to teach them to earn a living. They will be trained in head, hand, and heart; their heads to think, their hands to work, and their hearts to have faith."[11]

At Daytona Beach a number of very wealthy men had their winter homes. Mrs. Bethune went to some of them to ask for help. She trained her children in the Negro spirituals, and after a time she got them invited to some of the Daytona mansions to sing, and also to churches and to the resort hotels. "I had learned already," she said, "that one of my most important jobs was to be a good beggar! I rang doorbells and tackled cold prospects without a lead. I wrote articles for whoever would print them, distributed leaflets, rode interminable miles of dusty roads on my old bicycle, invaded churches, clubs, lodges, chambers of commerce. If a prospect refused to make a contribution I would say 'Thank you for your time.' No matter how deep my hurt, I always smiled. I refused to be discouraged, for neither God nor man can use a discouraged person."[12]

In less than two years the number of children in the school had grown to two hundred and fifty, with some volunteer workers and a few paid teachers, and another building was rented next door. But if only she could get a piece of land and put a building on it that the school would own! At the edge of the Negro section there was a piece of land—next to the city dump. It could be bought for two hundred dollars, five dollars down and the rest due in two years. She sold ice cream and pies she had made, accumulated five dollars, and took the small change, wrapped in her handkerchief, to the owner. Now at least she had something staked out for the future.

Then she began to think that her school ought to be organized. She wrote a letter to one of the rich men who, as she saw in the newspaper, had come to Daytona Beach. He answered the letter and told her to come to see him. She appealed to him to come and look at what she was doing—and would he be a trustee of her school? Yes, he would come and look. So he did drive around to Oak Street, walk in the door, and stare with astonishment at the crude rooms and the makeshift equipment inside.

"Where is the school you want me to be a trustee of?" he asked. Still in her imagination, she told him: waiting to be built.

To that gentleman, James N. Gamble of the Procter and Gamble firm, her earnestness made appeal. Also perhaps he and others like him saw in her, with admiration, the same boldness of adventure which made the great achievements in their business world. They did organize her school, became its trustees, and helped it to grow, by giving to it themselves and by telling their friends about it. The land Mrs. Bethune had bought was cleared, and by 1907 Faith Hall had been built upon it, partly with sand and secondhand bricks she had begged from contractors, and by work after hours by Negro workmen whose children she took into the school. Over the entrance to its four stories was inscribed: ENTER TO LEARN, and over that door within: DEPART TO SERVE.

Not long after that, her mother came to see her. "Janie, Janie," her mother cried as she was taken into the arms of the daughter who had been the little girl of the cabin and the cotton field; and Mary Bethune answered, "Mama, wait until you see my school. Wait until you see! I have nearly four hundred children; we're crowded but we're happy."[13]

Of course the days were not always happy. Notwithstanding the generous help which came from many friends, there were financial worries, bills that could not be paid on time, creditors who had to be persuaded please to wait. Also there was the latent antagonism of that part of the white people resentful of anything which would educate Negroes "clean out of their place, so that they won't want to be servants anymore." One night before an election day, to the terror of the children, the Ku-Klux Klan, white-robed, hooded, and carrying torches, marched in front of the school. "Turn on every light," commanded Mary Bethune. "Let them know we're home." And the next day she made her reply to their would-be intimidation. "I was standing at the polling place at eight o'clock with a line of Negroes behind me," she said. "They kept us waiting all day, but *we voted.*"[14]

The school kept growing. The ground which once had been the border of the dump was turned into two gardens, for flowers and for vegetables which many people in Daytona came to buy. More and better buildings were erected. By 1911 the school was teaching high school grades. Fourteen years later, Cookman Institute of Jacksonville, which had been educating Negro boys, was moved to Daytona and combined with Mrs. Bethune's school as the Daytona Cookman Collegiate Institute; and not long afterward, in honor of the woman who was its continuing inspiration, its name was changed to Bethune-Cookman College. Now that college has twenty-seven buildings, a faculty of more than one hundred, and more than one thousand students, 75 percent of whom go out to become teachers; and it has attained an "A" rating in the Southern Association of Colleges and Secondary Schools.

Nor was the creation of this school the only conspicuous service Mary Bethune rendered to the Negro people and to the whole nation of which they were and are a part. When President Franklin D. Roosevelt, coming into office in 1933, found the country in the depths of economic depression, one of his early acts was the creation of the National Youth Administration, and Mary McLeod Bethune was summoned to Washington to become Director of the Division of Negro Affairs in that National Youth Administration, the highest position in the government service then held by a Negro woman; and in the course of her work she was able to open the way to education or to employment for tens of thousands of Negro young men and women who otherwise would have been condemned to ignorance and uselessness. She organized the National Council of Negro Women, which became a country-wide force through which the needs of Negroes could be made known. At a mass meeting in New York she voiced the new hope and confidence which had come to her people. "Throughout the history of your life in this country—three hundred years," she said, "you have been regarded as a patient, submissive minority . . . chattels, like any horse, or plow or iron pot. . . . Then came your emancipation.

Still you were patient, experiencing discrimination, injustice, segregation, and denials of equal opportunities. . . . The pall of a slave experience still hung over the masses of our people. They had a right to speak out, but dared not speak. Today a new Negro has arisen in America. He is here tonight in Madison Square Garden. He is you!"[15]

The woman who had grown from the little girl of the Mayesville cabin had justified the faith which had been put in her. When she was speaking once to the National Council of Negro Women, in Los Angeles, there sat on the platform a quiet and shy old lady, Miss Mary Crissman, the person who out of her savings had given the scholarship which enabled Mary Jane McLeod to get her education. When Mary McLeod Bethune was handed an armful of flowers after her address that night, she turned and laid them in Miss Crissman's lap. "Invest in a human soul," she said to her audience. "Who knows? It might be a diamond in the rough."[16]

❧ IX ❧

Edith Cavell

Sometimes it may happen that a single life will epitomize a period of history so momentous that at the end of it one sees that the kind of world which existed at its beginning will never exist again.

In the vital statistics for December 4, 1865, in Swardeston, England, a hamlet of three hundred people, there was recorded the birth of a girl baby. Her name was Edith Cavell, the daughter of the vicar of that village parish. In her own self she might never have been notable; but the fateful drama of her time, moving with the dark inexorableness of a Greek tragedy, was to make her a symbol of forces greater than herself. At the end of a career which otherwise could only have seemed commonplace, she would represent in her death both the stark fact of human evil, and a glimpse of a light that may lead beyond the darkness.

When Edith Cavell was born, there was little sign, and certainly no general consciousness, that history was moving toward a catastrophic era. To be sure, there had been and there would be wars and disturbances here and there, but nothing that involved the whole world's peril. Notwithstanding temporary setbacks, it appeared that the life of civilized nations possessed not only stability but also an accumulated richness of achievement out of which all material and moral benefit would dependably grow. England was in the midst of what was to seem the almost fabulous Victorian era, when the British empire girdled the earth and the British navy ruled the seven seas. In Victoria's astonishing sixty-four years upon the throne, the population of Great Britain doubled, its wealth tripled, and its trade increased sixfold. During her reign she had become not only Queen of Great Britain, Scotland, Wales and Ireland, but also—both in name and in fact—the Empress of India. At her "Diamond Jubilee," in 1897, there marched in the glittering festival parade in London the troops not only from that great subcontinent, but from innumerable other colonies and dominions of an empire of which it could be said that "the sun never sets upon it," an empire which included one square mile out of every four on the surface of the earth, and one person out of five of the whole earth's population. Small wonder that in the eleventh edition of the *Encylopaedia Britannica* the editor-in-chief, writing the article on Queen Victoria, could find himself swept into a kind of exultancy which saw Victoria as "the greatest of English sovereigns, whose name would in history mark an age."

It would have seemed, therefore, at the turn of the century that for anyone born under the English flag life would certainly be safe and secure. And security seemed a wider fact than that. The ruling families of Europe were knit together by such an extraordinary complex of relationships radiating from Queen Victoria that many might have assumed complacently that no violent divisions could ensue. The Emperor of Germany was Victoria's grandson; the Empress of Russia was her granddaughter; the Princess Alexandra of Denmark was married to her son; and others of her nine children were linked by marriage to other principalities of Europe. Moreover, after the Queen's death in 1901, it still seemed to those who did not look too far beneath the surface that the *Pax Britannica* meant peace among the nations generally. Victoria was succeeded by her son, the Prince of Wales, who as Edward VII tried to establish strong ties with France; and under whom the British empire reached the peak of its prosperity and power. When he died in 1910, and nine kings came to his funeral, the crowds in London, "waiting in hushed and black-clad awe, could not keep back gasps of admiration. In scarlet and blue and green and purple, three by three the sovereigns rode through the palace gates, with plumed helmets, gold braid, crimson sashes, and jeweled orders flashing in the sun. After them came five heirs apparent, forty more imperial or royal highnesses, seven queens . . . and a scattering of special ambassadors from uncrowned countries. Together they represented seventy nations in the greatest assemblage of royal rank ever gathered in one place. . . ."[1]

While all these events were taking place, Edith Cavell was growing up unnoticed and almost unknown. As a little girl in the vicarage she would go with her mother to church where her father would read matins every morning, and back again for vespers in the evening. "He prayed with a doomsday ring, parishioners were to recall," which "'caused uneasy stirrings within them. . . . 'Rock of Ages' was among his favorite hymns, the Litany the penitential refrain for his own soul."[2] But he had a sense of duty toward his neighbor as well as toward God, and when there was some infrequent luxury on the vicarage dining table he would share it with the needy villagers. The thoughtful gray-eyed daughter was to reflect both aspects of her father, a seriousness of spirit that was almost somber, but at the same time a sensitive compassion for those who might look to her for help. At first her father tutored her and her sister in his study at the vicarage, but later he managed out of his slender stipend to send her to school in Peterborough, under the shadow of the cathedral. Grown to be a young woman, she went to Belgium for five happy years as governess for the four children of a Brussels lawyer named François; and the children were to remember always her kindness and patience, and "her veritable horror of lying."[3]

In 1895 she returned to England because her father was ill, and the next year she determined to study to be a nurse. Florence Nightingale had lifted nursing into something efficient and medically respected not many years before, but it was still carried on under such bleak conditions and so poorly rewarded that only women of exceptional devotion were likely to take it up. Edith Cavell was first a probationer at London Hospital on

Whitechapel Road, at the edge of the grimy and poverty-stricken East End. After two years' experience, she was given supervision over a group of nurses and sent to combat an outbreak of typhoid fever in Kent. Next she became assistant matron at the Shoreditch Infirmary, and then matron of a District Home in the industrial city of Manchester. A Mrs. Annie Kent, one of those who knew her there, remembered her as

> an angel of mercy to the poor, the sick, the injured. . . .
> I can see her now, . . . her cape and black bag, hurrying through the streets of Manchester. People would look up and say, "There goes nurse Cavell!"
> She was very kind to the poor or anybody who needed help. She nursed them all. . . .
> In addition to the mills, there were mines outside of Manchester and I can remember nurse Cavell being first on the scene to help when there was an explosion or accident. After she left, they called her the "poor man's Nightingale" in Manchester, and her picture was in almost every house.[4]

Three years before the death of Edward VII, Edith Cavell, now an experienced and able nurse, was back in Belgium—a Belgium which was destined soon to become fatefully different from the light-hearted country she had known before. A brilliant Brussels surgeon, impatient, hot-tempered, and indignant at the low standards both of medicine and nursing in his country, had opened a clinic and planned to open also a nurses' training school. Through the François family, he learned of Edith Cavell, and invited her to come from England and organize his nurses' school. Previously, nursing in Belgium had been almost wholly the province of nuns; and through ignorance and bigotry, nurses who had not taken the church's vows were looked upon as atheists, and of doubtful morals. But Dr. Antoine Depage and Edith Cavell, who was now the directress in his clinic, were bent upon creating an institution which would be its own sufficient argument. As Miss Cavell wrote to the *Nursing Mirror* in London, "The contrast the probationers present to the nuns in their grimy apparel is the contrast of the unhygienic past with the enlightened present. These Belgium probationers in three years' time will look back on the first days of trial with wonder. . . . [They] have good will, courage, and perseverance. They will show their countrywomen that education and position do not constitute a bar to an independent life." She wanted to make clear to young girls of the more privileged class that "work is not a social stigma," and that the nursing profession could have a dignity deserving "all of their devotion and their efforts."[5]

The great gathering of sovereigns and other representatives from many nations at the funeral of Edward VII in 1910 gave, in its splendid show, the impression of a world bound together by sympathy and shared purpose. But it could conceal only for the moment the deep currents of rivalry and danger that ran beneath the seeming concord. As, in the descriptive words already remembered, it was "the greatest assemblage of royalty and rank ever gathered in one place," so also it was "of its kind, the last. The muffled tongue of Big Ben tolled nine by the clock as the cortege left the palace, but on history's clock it was sunset, and the sun of the old world was setting in a dying blaze of splendor never to be seen again." Later, when the body of the king was escorted to Paddington Station to go by train to Windsor for burial, "the Royal Horse Guards' band played the 'Dead March' from *Saul*. Lord Esher wrote in his diary after the funeral: 'There never was such a break-up. All the old buoys which have marked the channel of our lives seem to have been swept away.' "[6]

Four years later the whole structure of what had seemed to be a world at peace began to crumble like a falling wall. Austria-Hungary attacked Serbia; Germany, Russia, and France mobilized; Germany violated the neutrality of Belgium; England entered the conflict, and by the early autumn of 1914 all Europe was at war. At the moment, Edith Cavell was in England, where she had gone for a summer visit to her mother. Prudence and reason would have seemed to dictate that she should stay there. But emotional attachment to her work in Brussels and loyalty to her nurses drew her back. She boarded a crowded channel steamer to Ostend, and reached Brussels to find the city in a fever of excitement as detachments of the half-trained army marched through the streets to face the German columns which had already crossed the Belgian border.

It was not long before most of Belgium had been overrun. On August 17, the Belgian government fled to Antwerp. On the 20th the invaders entered Brussels. For the Belgian people, outraged and embittered, the German columns represented nothing but embodied evil, "a gray horde of goose-stepping, almost mechanized creatures." It is the nature of war to produce its undiscriminating hatreds, to see everything in the absolute opposites of black and white, and to recognize in the enemy nothing that is not altogether of the Devil. It was the more remarkable therefore that Edith Cavell, identified though she was with the Belgian people, could still be sensitive to the individual decencies of human nature which an evil militarism perverts in its mass cruelty, but cannot wholly destroy. On August 21 she wrote:

> Many more troops came through; from our road we could see the long procession and when the halt was called at mid-day and carts came up with supplies, some were too weary to eat, and slept on the pavement of the street.

> We were divided between pity for these poor fellows, far from their country and their people, suffering the weariness and fatigue of an arduous campaign—and hate of a cruel and vindictive foe bringing ruin and desolation on hundreds of happy homes and to a prosperous and peaceful land. Some of the Belgians spoke to the invaders in German and found they were very vague as to their whereabouts, and imagined they were already in Paris; they were surprised to be speaking

to Belgians and could not understand what quarrel they had with them.

I saw several of the men pick up little children and give them chocolate or seat them on their horses, and some had tears in their eyes at the recollection of the little ones at home.[7]

But though Edith Cavell thus could be aware that the tragedy and pathos of war is not confined to one side in any struggle, this was far from meaning that she was bogged down in any sentimental neutrality of judgment. When the German grip had been clamped down on Belgium, she wrote: "I have seen suffering, poverty, and human wretchedness in the slums of London, but nothing I saw there hurts me the way it does to see these proud, gay, happy people humiliated and deprived of their men, their homes invaded by enemy soldiers that are quartered in them, their business ruined. I can only ask myself why, oh why, should these innocent people be made to suffer like this?" And when she was cautioned not to be too outspoken, she answered, "In times like these, when terror makes might seem right, there is a higher duty than prudence."[8]

There was another voice in Belgium which did not stop with prudence. Before the war was over and while the German power was still unbroken, Cardinal Mercier of Malines would write to the Governor General who controlled the occupation: "But there is a barrier before which military force is held up and behind which is intrenched inviolate right. On this side of the barrier it is we, the representatives of moral authority, who speak as masters. . . . We will wait in patience for the day of retaliation, not retaliation on this earth, however; that we have already, for the occupation regime you have forced upon us is abhorred by everybody in the world who has any sense of honor. I speak of the verdict of history; I speak of the inevitable judgment of the God of Justice."[9] The archbishop's eminence made the Germans not quite dare to touch him. Edith Cavell had no such safeguard. She made no pronouncements; but she

had the quiet and inflexible courage to do what was bound to
bring punishment as surely as any pronouncement could. She
made the hospital over which she was now presiding a refuge
for allied soldiers trying to escape. An underground network
directed these men to Brussels. Other secret helpers would get
the men—or some of them—across the border into Holland,
beyond the German reach. Meanwhile for the harborage she
furnished, Edith Cavell, and her nurses with her, were in constant jeopardy.

By the summer of 1915 the German police were keeping 149
Rue de la Culture under increasing surveillance. Also, they were
closing the net around some of those who belonged to the underground through which escape of those who had been sheltered at
the hospital was made possible. In the Avenue de Roodebeek in
Brussels was the house of Philippe Baucq. He was one of the
little group who produced and distributed the clandestine paper
La Libre Belgique. Once a week it appeared, as if from nowhere,
to the fury and frustration of the occupying power, and a copy
of it turned up with insulting regularity on the desk of the
German Governor General himself. By trailing a suspected visitor, the police found their way to Baucq's house, and when they
broke into it, they found not only a stack of the newly printed
issue of *La Libre Belgique*, but also incriminating letters, including one from Edith Cavell.

Now the police descended upon the hospital. The rooms
were searched, and Edith Cavell and her first assistant, Elizabeth
Wilkins, arrested and carried off to police headquarters. After
a grueling examination which she parried adroitly, Sister Wilkins was released, but Miss Cavell was taken by the secret
police to St. Gilles Prison, an enormous grim city, "fanning out
like the gray spokes of a monster wheel, [which] foreboded only
gloom once its massive oak and iron gates closed."[10]

It was on August 5, 1915, that she was arrested. The American
Embassy, to which British interests in Belgium had been committed, tried to have the lawyer Georges de Leval accepted as
her defending counsel, but the Germans refused to admit him

to the prison. Miss Cavell was kept from outside contacts, except that she was allowed to send a letter to one of her nurses. In it she wrote: "I am afraid you will not be able to come and see me at present. But you can write, only your letter will be read."[11]

On Friday, October 8, Edith Cavell and thirty-three others, including Philippe Baucq, were brought to trial. She refused to deny or seek to extenuate anything that she had done. Yes, she had received into the hospital, and shielded, and helped on their way to escape, allied soldiers and young Belgians of military age; it was her duty, she said, to save their lives. She would make no plea to her German judges. With proud dignity, she told the whole truth, even though it added to their indictment.

"Do you think these men you helped to escape were grateful for what you did?" the prosecutor asked.

"I know that they were grateful," she answered.

"How do you know?"

"Because they wrote to me, some of them from England, to thank me that they had arrived." Arrived in England: which meant that they could fight for England against Germany again. For the woman on trial, that was an ominous fact. The prosecutor summed up his case. On Monday, October 11, the prisoners were brought before their judges to hear their verdicts.

It was a bleak day, with a cold rain falling. Few people were in the streets. The nurses in the hospital had finished a scanty supper, and like the rest of Brussels were trying to keep warm. Through the window they saw the figure of a man, clutching his coat collar to keep out the rain, hurrying up the walk. It was Monsieur H. K. Van Halteren, one of the directors of the hospital. One look at his face was enough to show that he brought calamitous news. Miss Cavell had been condemned to death. She would be executed in the morning at five o'clock.

Elizabeth Wilkins and another one of the nurses flung their capes about them and went out into the rain—to the gate of St. Gilles Prison first, where they learned nothing; then to the house of M. de Leval. The clock had struck eight. If anything were to be accomplished before the morning, it had to be with agonizing haste. "I will go to the United States minister at once," said M. de Leval, and with the two nurses he hastened to the American Embassy. The American ambassador was ill, but Hugh Gibson, the secretary, was found. He got hold of the Spanish ambassador, and those two, with M. de Leval, drove to the headquarters of the German political ministry. The house was dark—no answer to their furious ringing of the bell. They pounded on the door; finally a sulky concierge appeared. "No one home."

"Where is Baron von der Lancken?" Hugh Gibson demanded.

"At the theater," the concierge informed them.

Well, they would come in and wait while the concierge in their car should go and carry to von der Lancken their urgent message.

It was after half-past ten when von der Lancken returned, and two aides with him. What was all the excitement about? Why not go home reasonably and sleep and come back tomorrow?

The three visitors answered angrily. A woman's life was at stake, and the clock was ticking off the minutes before the morning.

"The life of one German soldier seems to us much more important than that of all the old English nurses," said one of the insolent German aides; and von der Lancken added irritably, "It is past eleven o'clock. What can be done? *Nichts!*"[12]

But Hugh Gibson and the Spanish ambassador pressed him with a determination that would not be shaken off. They prevailed upon him to go to see the military governor, von Sauberzweig. He went—and they waited, while the hands of the clock moved on. Ten minutes to twelve. Five minutes. Then von der Lancken returned. "The Military Governor has decided the infliction of the death penalty is imperative," he answered. "I am exceedingly sorry, but he will not change his decision."[13]

The two ambassadors and M. de Leval put on their coats, and with no parting word or gesture to disguise the anger and contempt they felt, walked out of the ministry door into the dark and empty night.

Meanwhile, in St. Gilles Prison a British chaplain, the Rev. H. S. T. Gahan, responding to a message, had gone to see Miss Cavell. A jailer opened the door of her cell and let him in. She rose to meet him. "I have no fear nor shrinking," she said. "I have seen death so often it is not strange or fearful to me. I expected it would end thus. I thank God for this ten weeks' quiet before the end."

"They have all been very kind to me here," she continued. "But this I would say, standing as I do in view of God and eternity. I realize that patriotism is not enough. I must have no hatred or bitterness toward anyone."

The Rev. Mr. Gahan read the service of Holy Communion, and administered to her the bread and wine; and at the end the two of them said together:

> Abide with me; fast falls the eventide,
> The darkness deepens; Lord, with me abide;
> When other helpers fail, and comforts flee,
> Help of the helpless, O abide with me.[14]

The next morning about daybreak two gray military sedans rolled out through the gates of St. Gilles Prison, bound for the rifle range at the *Tir National*. In one of them, flanked by armed guards, was Edith Cavell. Arriving at the *Tir National*, she carried her Prayer Book in her hand, and wrote in it one final note: "Died at 7 A.M. on October 12th, 1915. With love to my mother. E. Cavell." Then she faced the German firing squad, and was shot down.

She had fulfilled the promise she had made to her mother in a letter written when the German armies first stormed over Belgium. "I shall think of you to the last, and you may be sure we shall do our duty here and die as women of our race should die."[15]

In May, 1919, the body of Edith Cavell, which had been buried where she was shot, was taken on a British destroyer to

England, carried by a special train to London, and through streets packed with people to a memorial service in Westminster Abbey, and then interred again in the shadow of Norwich Cathedral, in that part of England where she had been born.

Near Trafalgar Square, at the heart of London, stands her statue, and on its pedestal are these words which she spoke to the chaplain as he gave her Communion on the night before her execution: "Patriotism is not enough. I must have no hatred or bitterness toward anyone."

Patriotism, the love of one's own country and willingness to serve it, can be a great and noble thing. But, as Edith Cavell understood, it is not enough. If it is passionate and blind, and sees no further than "my country, right or wrong," it can lead to cruel evil. If mankind is to be saved from war and ultimate destruction, there must be something more than patriotism. There must be a larger vision of all humanity which recognizes that the ultimate good for one's own country must be forever bound up with what is good for all the peoples of the earth.

✣ X ✣

Mary-Cooke Branch Munford

In the winter of 1865 the War between the States was drawing near to what would be, for the men and women of the Confederacy, its tragic end. After fierce and inconclusive fighting in the previous summer at Spotsylvania and Cold Harbor, Virginia, General Grant had abandoned his frontal assault on Richmond, the capital of the Confederacy, and had swung the Union army east and south of Richmond and laid siege to Petersburg, twenty miles away. Not only the breastworks around the city, but the city itself was under fire. The sound of the cannonading shook the windows of the house on Tabb Street where Martha Louise Patteson Branch, the young wife of Colonel James Read Branch of the Confederate Army, was living with her four small children. It seemed to be time to move.

In Richmond lived Dr. William A. Patteson, Mrs. Branch's father. Since the beginning of the war, Richmond, attacked again and again, might not have been chosen as an isle of safety; but now it seemed less unsafe than Petersburg. So the old doctor's daughter with her four children came home to the house where she had lived as a girl and in which she had been married eight years before. From its front windows on Broad Street one could get glimpses of the Capitol Square and in its center the pillared Capitol, designed by Thomas Jefferson, where the Legislature of Virginia had met since 1788, and where from 1861 till 1865 the Confederate Congress had its seat.

Dr. Patteson was too old for service in the army, but like other physicians of his age he had worked in the makeshift hospitals of Richmond into which flowed the ghastly tide of wounded from the desperate fighting which sometimes was so near that it could be heard from streets of the city. James Read Branch had begun his service in the Confederacy as captain of a company of infantry which he had recruited. Transferred to the artillery, at the battle of Malvern Hill, when nearly all his men had been killed, he himself served one of his two remaining guns, and managed to get both of them away when he was ordered to retire. Badly wounded later, he lay for a long time in a military hospital, but he had recovered and was still in service. Martha Branch, living as all the young wives of her generation did in the knowledge that any morning the casualty lists which lengthened after every battle might hold the name she dreaded to see, had in her a passion of loyalty which gave to her thoughts a color that they never lost. To her the Confederate cause was sacred, lifted above all questioning in the fierce devotion which identified it with the two men she loved best. Dr. Patteson, grave and gentle, was also resolute; James Branch was fiery tempered and masterful; but she had the ardor which can make women in wartime, denied the release of actual fighting, more formidable in their stored-up passion than their men. For her there were convictions which were absolute, and for which no devotion could be too great. Some of that intensity of spirit was to be passed on to her children, and not least to the child who as the war moved on into its last fateful months was being carried in her body. This child, a daughter, was born on September 16, 1865, and christened in St. Paul's Church as Mary-Cooke.

In what manner and to what degree the nature of a child may be affected by the emotions of its mother no one can be wise enough to fathom; but the little daughter of Martha Branch could hardly have been untouched by the shadows that fell upon her mother's world beginning in the year when she was born. In April there came the shattering fact of the Confederacy's defeat. General Robert E. Lee's lines at Petersburg were broken, and Richmond lay defenseless. The next day, past the windows of the house on Broad Street, marched the victorious northern army, while black smoke billowed into the sky from the lower end of the city where warehouses had been set on fire. The cause that men and women had fought and suffered for through the four years of war was dead.

And there was to be another death. In 1869 came the first opportunity for the people of Virginia to vote for a governor after the military occupation. James Branch threw himself into the effort to elect a moderate and reconciling man. As the campaign mounted in intensity, his wife—as with a premonition—said to him. "You will never live to the end of this." On the morning of July 2, as he left the house she said, "I have a feeling you will never come back." He kissed her and laughed. "You have been saying that all this time, and now the campaign is over. This is the last day." As he went to organize a rally of voters on an island in the James River, a wooden bridge collapsed and he was thrown into the water. Many men tried to save him, including a Negro who himself was badly hurt; but they could not get him free from the fallen timbers. That afternoon he was brought home dead.

The four-year-old daughter shared the family grief in such measure as a child can. But children are resilient. There was Dr. Patteson to lavish affection upon her, and there were children to play with, and all the happy kaleidoscope of a little girl's concerns. Nevertheless, somewhere in her subconsciousness was the awareness that life can be very formidable, and that it may bring great burdens which one must be brave enough to bear.

As the years went by, and she had been to school and was on the threshold of young womanhood, she was in deep ways like her mother, and yet different too. She had her mother's loyalties: to the memory of her father, to Virginia, to the causes and the people he had loved. In a brief personal sketch which at a later time she wrote at the request of the editor of a volume of biographies, she included this: "As a child I helped in the Confederate Bazaar, and went each year with my mother to

decorate the soldiers' graves in Hollywood."¹ She did not want
to forget the things that were past; and she knew that she could
not, even if she wanted to. But she did tremendously want not
only the Old South, but a New South. She had not thought
out yet what that might involve, but her face was set in the
direction that might lead to it—in the direction of independence,
of imagination, of experiment not too easily made afraid. She felt
that there was a debt which everybody had to pay to all the great
tradition which the South had handed on; but a new generation
was rising, and it might pay that debt by something better than
decorating soldiers' graves.

New ideas, however, were not popular in Richmond among
"the best people." There was much wonderment and shaking
of heads when it was learned that Mary-Cooke Branch and some
of the other girls of her group had established a club for working girls in two rooms which they had rented in a little house
on Main Street. She did this because of her sense of responsibility
for girls who had fewer advantages than she had and because of
her spontaneous desire to widen her own sympathy and understanding through knowing them. Such books and magazines as
the founders of the club could get hold of were put in the
club rooms, and the girls met there to play games and talk and
discuss. But what did these girls discuss? the elders were asking.
And what upsetting notions might be in their heads?

About Mary-Cooke Branch, the chief cause for consternation
among her acquaintances was not the founding of the club for
working girls, but something further. She wanted to go to
college. That was being "strong-minded" to a degree that made
Richmond society gasp. To go to college was something that
simply "was not done" by southern women. There might be
women's colleges somewhere, but they could be disposed of as
"only a Yankee notion." That was the feeling which Mrs. James
Branch shared. She could not believe that a daughter of hers
wanted to do anything so unfeminine. If Mary-Cooke went, it
would be over her indignant protest.

Here was a crisis in the girl's life which tested her character

as profoundly as anything else she would ever be called upon
to face. She wanted to go to college with a consuming eagerness,
and the strong will which she had already shown to be hers
rebelled against an obstacle put in her way. She knew she could
go if she determined to; from her father's will enough income
had come to her to make her financially independent. But she
saw that her going would make an emotional breach with her
mother which might never be healed. The tragedy for her in
the dilemma was the more acute because it seemed so needless.
Fundamentally, her mother should have understood and shared
her longing. Her mother's mind was quick and keen, as hers
was. Her mother loved to read, and could discuss alertly what
she had read. If her mother had been born into her generation,
she was the very type who would have wanted to go to college
herself. But she had been born into a time which wove its
restrictions upon women into the closest fabric of its family
affections. Certain suppositions about what a woman should or
should not do were identified for Martha Patteson Branch with
the men to whom she had been devoted, with the old society
she had loved and seen destroyed, with a complex of loyalties
so much deeper than reasoning that they could be unreasonably
hurt.

Her daughter sensed all this through the years of her mature
girlhood. She clung wistfully to her hope of college; but she
knew at last that she would never gain her mother's consent. So
she deliberately gave up the one ambition which she most
passionately cherished. One day when she was visiting her
closest friend she came into the room with a letter in her hand.
She flung herself with bitter weeping on the bed. "I have
decided," she sobbed. "College is gone!"

Many other young women have had equal distresses. Others
have wanted to go to college and could not go. Mary-Cooke
Branch therefore was not exceptional in the fact of facing
grievous disappointment. What was exceptional in her was the
way in which she turned that disappointment into enlargement
of the outreach of her life. If she could not have the opportunities

she had coveted for herself, she would try to see that others had them. To the end of her life she would be fighting on many fronts to improve the schools, and to open roads to college for all eager young people, especially the girls of Virginia and the South. In this she was fortified by the great enrichment of her life, her marriage to Beverley Bland Munford, brilliant young lawyer in Richmond, who like herself had a romantic devotion to what Virginia had been, and yet was not shackled by its past. She was twenty-two when he first saw her at a crowded reception, standing at its border and regarding—as he wrote afterward—"with rather unapproving eyes the prospect before her. There was about her an air of mingled diffidence and audacity." He fell in love with her, and for seven years he pressed his suit. Although she liked and admired him, she was not sure at first that she wanted to marry anybody; but at last she realized that she needed him, as he had long been sure he needed her. Their marriage in 1893 promised the fulfillment of everything that had meant most to her. They were congenial in ways that went both wide and deep. They had similar traditions and loyalties, and at the same time his impulses were liberal and forward-looking, as hers were. Their tastes were alike both in their home and in the world outside. They loved books and they loved music. He was handsome and gay and buoyant, and she had great beauty in face and figure and in her soprano voice. Warm circles of friendship surrounded them when they had established their home, first in a little house on Monroe Park and then in one of spacious dignity which had been built in 1842 on the site of a still earlier house where George Wythe, the first Chancellor of Virginia had studied law. The birth of two children rounded their family life; and beyond the home their interests reached out into civic affairs together.

One of the first ventures which attracted Mary-Cooke Munford—with her husband's encouragement—was an enterprise which most Richmonders regarded with skepticism if not with suspicion, namely, the organization of a Woman's Club. At that time only a very few cities here and there in the whole of

America possessed one. No such thing existed in Richmond society, or ever had. What would ladies be meeting outside their own homes for, and how could propriety and such an "outrageous and unwomanly" notion as forming a Woman's Club go together? That was what most of the ladies, and still more of their husbands, wanted to know. But a little group of women who thought for themselves, only fourteen at first, determined that a Woman's Club was what they wanted; and not only that, it was also, they thought, what Richmond needed. "All we did for amusement then," said one of them, "was to go to entertainments, get up late, and take it easy. But many of us who had travelled and studied were anxious for a center where we might exchange ideas."[2]

Among the organizers, Mary-Cooke Munford was the youngest; but from the start she was one of the moving spirits. In the beginning the club was lodged in rented rooms. But after a few years, when she had been elected president, there came upon the real-estate market a fine old large-room residence—the very house, she thought, that the club should have. So she set to work to stir up the will to get it. The club had less than a thousand dollars in its treasury, and when she went to Richmond bankers to borrow twenty thousand dollars, they smiled after her with amused incredulity as they bowed her empty-handed from their offices. But through the help of one businessman more forward-looking than the general lot, she got the money—from a bank in Baltimore. The house was bought, the club grew to a membership of over a thousand, with two hundred on its waiting list, and became the most important influence in Richmond for the cultural stimulus of the leading women of the city. As far as her leadership could carry it, she constantly tried to widen its concerns—not withstanding the fact that once in the early years when she tried to stir the club to active interest in certain important civic matters affecting Richmond, the members showed their disapproval by knocking with their umbrellas on the floor.

But her interest was not centered in activities for her own

social group. She and her husband together had two much larger concerns: one was the public school system, which touched the great body of Virginia boys and girls; the other was a fairer chance for the weakest and most disadvantaged group in the community, the Negroes.

The public school system of Virginia at the beginning of the century so far as Negro children were concerned was pitiable, and for white children not vastly better. As late as 1905, though the superintendent of public instruction in Virginia must be an "experienced educator," his salary was only two thousand dollars a year, with no more than four hundred dollars annually for traveling expenses. Most of the rural schools were primitive one-room affairs. Many of the buildings even in a city such as Richmond were ugly and ill-kept. Salaries of teachers were beggarly, and the standards of required training low. The worst of it was that the general public did not seem to care.

But a renaissance was beginning. A few devoted leaders were proclaiming that "every child has the same right to be educated as he has to be free." From 1898 each year for two decades there was held the Conference for Education in the South. "It was there," wrote Mary-Cooke Munford, "that I realized the magnitude and importance of the educational problem in the South as it touched both the white people and the Negroes. The major interests of my life then took form, education for all the people, fostering better knowledge and understanding between the races, and especially the rebuilding of my mother state, Virginia."

In 1901 she helped to found the Richmond Education Association, the first organized effort in the city to enlist its people for the improvement of the public schools. From 1904 to 1911 she was its president. Through public meetings, through the newspapers, and through leaflets of its own (the money for which she mostly raised), the Association led an increasing number of citizens to make up their minds that something more aggressive had to be done in and for the public schools, and this lit the kind of fire of public opinion which is the only thing that is certain to make office-holders move. The school authorities were galvanized into larger plans for both the curriculum and the fabric of the schools. Mrs. Munford gathered funds to pay the first costs of industrial training in one of the Negro schools, and persuaded the school board to introduce it; from which beginning industrial education and manual arts were extended through the whole city system.

But the Richmond Education Association had of course a limited field. Outside Richmond there were the wider and more crying needs of the whole state. One of the men whose great spirit responded to these was Dr. Hollis B. Frissell, head of Hampton Institute. Coming unostentatiously to Richmond, he invited to his hotel room a little group to talk together about might best be done to improve Virginia schools, to overcome the backward conditions of many kinds which cramped the life of rural districts, and to develop a public sentiment for social and educational advance in the whole Commonwealth. Out of that meeting came the founding in 1903 of the Co-operative Education Association of Virginia, and in the period from 1910 to 1925 Mary-Cooke Munford was its president. The word "co-operative" in its title was indicative of the width of its purpose and the scope of the forces it sought to rally. It must bring together in mutual knowledge and related effort all the constructive agencies which otherwise might have been working in their own little separated grooves. To build a decent schoolhouse, to staff it with properly trained teachers, and to keep it open for an adequate term—that obviously was the first educational need in every neighborhood. But sick children could not come to school, and children with poor eyesight or other physical defects could not do good work; so what about public health and the ways and means for improvement? Roads which in the winter got deep in mud or blocked with snow cut down school attendance as well as disrupting neighborhood contacts generally. What about the

State Highway Commission, and what it could be made to do for country roads? Many of the families the children came from were uninformed and backward. What could be done to enable the schools to bring them together for entertainment and to wake them up with stimulating addresses and discussions? Many of the homes in the country were drab and crude and uncomfortable, and much of the farming was done so unscientifically that thousands of the people were always poor. What could be done to teach fathers of school children how to manage their farming better and mothers to make more attractive homes?

All those questions the Association not only asked but tried to answer. As its president, Mrs. Munford brought to it the great gift of imaginative planning and also of steady routine devotion. She had the vision to see unlimited possibilities for the Association's work; but she knew that these could be achieved only by patient and inconspicuous attention to detail. Franklin K. Lane, Secretary of the Interior in President Woodrow Wilson's cabinet, wrote to her: "The thing that so impresses me with your work is that it is so sensible, that you do not waste time with the discussion of vague theories, . . . but get right down to the one big job of the world, making the home and the home town and all its parts better to look at and live in and work with."[3] And when she resigned the presidency, the Board of Directors summed up her service: "The scope of the Association has been widened to embrace agriculture, public health, good roads, more practical churches, and community life in all its phases. . . . It is not an overstatement to say that every child in Virginia is better off because of Mrs. Munford's work."[4]

So for her the years after her marriage were full of exciting interests which brought the whole range of her abilities into play, in all of which she had the constant reinforcement of her husband's spirit. But then a shadow fell. Six years after their marriage it became evident that something had happened to Beverley Munford. A cough to which he had not paid much attention became more pronounced. The two of them went to New York to consult a specialist. He told Mary-Cooke Munford that her husband had tuberculosis. She should take him home and make him comfortable. He said he might live a year.

Now began the need for all her courage and for all Beverley Munford's buoyancy. Her life and energy would center now in fending off the doctor's prophecy. Instead of surrendering, she mobilized all her imagination and her inventiveness to shape the life of the family in such way as would hold out most promise for his benefit. For periods of time he was able to carry on his work in the law firm of which he was senior partner. One year she took him to Colorado Springs where he seemed to grow stronger, and another time to Arizona. She kept him alive not the one year only which the doctor had predicted, but eleven years, and in that time he had shared, sometimes actively and always with his full sympathy, in all that she had done in the name of them both.

Little by little, though, his physical strength faded. In the spring of 1910, in Richmond, he died. As Mary-Cooke Munford stood by his open grave, James Branch Cabell, her nephew, put into her hand this which he had written:

> Most blithe and sage and gentle, and most brave!
> O true clear heart, so quick to wake and war
> Against despondency, lest questioning mar
> One hour of living, or foiled hopes enslave
> And sour another's living! not to the grave
> Did we relinquish you, whose mourners were
> As mariners that mark, with hushed demur,
> Night's lordliest star sink in the insatiate wave,
> And so elude us, only to arise
> Elsewhere, with equal lustre—even as thus
> Today, unfearingly, in Paradise,
> And near the inmost court of Heaven's house,
> A gentleman to God lifts those brave eyes
> Which yesterday made life more brave for us.[5]

Before Beverley Munford died in 1910, Mrs. Munford had taken up a cause which for the next ten years she served with a devotion the more unflagging because she felt that his spirit went with her in all she sought to do.

One of the great southerners of his generation, Walter Hines Page, in an address which he gave in 1897, had said: "A public-school system generously supported by public sentiment, and generously maintained by both state and local taxation, is the only effective means to develop the forgotten man, and even more surely the only means to develop the forgotten woman."[6] Mary-Cooke Munford's long service on behalf of public education had made her acutely conscious of "the forgotten woman." By 1910 the newly established high schools of Virginia were graduating each year about twelve hundred pupils, and of these three-fifths were girls. If some of these girls were thirsty for more education, where could they go? If they had money enough, they could go to one of the women's colleges in the North: Vassar, Radcliffe, Mount Holyoke, Wellesley, Smith, Bryn Mawr; but for the great majority of them, a venture which required as much money as that seemed no more possible than a trip to the moon. Well then, they could go to one of the privately mantained colleges of Virginia, to Sweet Briar or to Randolph-Macon in Lynchburg, but even the more moderate charges at these were beyond their reach. What they needed was a state-supported college, as the climax to the state-supported schools in a "complete system of general instruction" which Thomas Jefferson had conceived as reaching "every description of our citizens from the richest to the poorest."[7]

But there was no state-supported college open to women. For the boys there were the University of Virginia and the College of William and Mary besides the Virginia Polytechnic Institute and the Virginia Military Institute. For the girls there was nothing but four normal schools, no one of them of collegiate rank, meant for the training of those girls who intended to teach in the public schools, but not preparing them to teach in anything higher than elementary grades. A high school teacher wrote in a letter to one of the Richmond newspapers: "In my twelve years high school experience, with twenty-four graduating classes, I have known only twice that a boy took the highest honors in his class. I have known this to happen repeatedly—a boy (averaging 86-89 per cent) to be valedictorian and carry off the University of Virginia scholarship, while a girl (average 95 per cent) and perhaps three other girls (above 90 per cent) would get nothing from the state at all."[8]

To Mary-Cooke Munford that was not an abstract matter. In her travels about Virginia, and in her visits to city and rural schools, she met girls who wanted to go to college and could not go, and into their longing she read vicariously the memory of her own. In one of the rare self-revelations found among her letters, she wrote once to a friend who had expressed his appreciation of her service to the schools, "Education has been my deepest interest from my girlhood, beginning with an almost passionate desire for the best in education for myself, which was denied because it was not the custom for girls in my class to receive a college education at that time. This interest has grown with my growth and strengthened with each succeeding year of my life."[9]

For her, the "passionate longing" which had been denied the college education it sought had nevertheless found at least a partial satisfaction in other ways: financial independence, travel, books, and a multitude of stimulating friendships and activities had given her the breadth of interest which she had wanted to go to college in order to get. But she knew that the vast majority of Virginia girls who looked wistfully toward college and then had to turn their eyes away would never have the other opportunities she had had. They would drop as untrained workers into the groove of petty tasks; or they would marry early, and although finding in many cases happiness that way, yet even in relative happiness never quite lose the hidden sense of frustration over what they had not gained for themselves and could not give to their husbands and their children.

So in one of the last months of Beverley Munford's life, Mary-Cooke Munford gathered together in their house a little group of women and a few men also whose interests she knew, and suggested that they see what they could do toward the establishment of a Co-ordinate College for Women at the University of Virginia. Their thought was that this proposed college for women should have its own individuality, its own organization and inner life, its own social, residence, and instruction halls; but should share—like Radcliffe College in its connection with Harvard—the library and laboratories of the university, and have among the members of its faculty some of the distinguished professors who were teaching the men. Thus the Co-ordinate College for Women would be no inferior and uncertain thing, but an integral part of the university which Jefferson had envisaged as for the education of all the people.

Edwin A. Alderman, president of the University of Virginia, said to its governing board: "My own judgment causes me to favor unreservedly the establishment by the State of a college for the education of women, and its location near the University of Virginia under its direction and control. . . . If we reject this opportunity, it seems to me that we deliberately adopt a policy of restricted effort and restricted ambition." And Woodrow Wilson, then President of the United States and himself a former student at the University of Virginia, wrote to Mrs. Munford: "The plans you have in mind for a Co-ordinate College at the University of Virginia seem to me thoroughly worthy of consideration and support."[10]

A bill for the establishment of the college was introduced in the State Legislature in 1910, but got nowhere. Mrs. Munford and her fellow workers bent to their task with new determination: to rally sentiment for the college that might be compelling when the Legislature met again.

But the opposition had also begun to gather, and it was to afford a curious revelation of the emotions which are roused when a new idea collides with the entrenched conservatisms of an old society. Some of the influential graduates of the University of Virginia sounded the alarm that the traditions of the university were in danger. They called mass meetings of the alumni in Richmond, Norfolk, Petersburg, Lynchburg, and other cities to organize protests to the Legislature. Most of these meetings promptly voted that no such thing as a college for women should be established in Charlottesville, lest it "destroy the spirit and character of the University." Here was the mind of the Southern Conservative who, as he was characterized by Professor Edwin Mims of Vanderbilt University in *The Advancing South*, is "honest, attractive, and most assuredly powerful" but who "takes for granted all his premises and swears to his conclusions . . . and brings heat rather than light to a discussion." Speakers against the college perhaps had not heard the words and certainly did not share the thoughts of a veteran of the War between the States, Senator Ben Hill, who in the year after General Robert E. Lee died said at the University of Georgia: "We live in one of those rare junctures in human affairs when one civilization ends and another begins. I feel oppressed with a sense of fear that we shall not be equal to the unusual responsibilities which this condition imposes, unless we can deal frankly with these events, frankly with ourselves, and bravely with our very habits of thought."[11]

No evidence which the advocates of the Co-ordinate College could bring as to what co-ordinate colleges actually were and as to what they had contributed to the wider usefulness of other universities could shake the emotional fixation of those who did not want anything different at the University of Virginia. Some of those who appeared at committee hearings of the Legislature dwelt in a world of insulated ideas and spoke a language that sounded hollow in the twentieth century. Said one fervent alumnus, if any College for Women comes near the University of Virginia, "that ancient republic will have ceased to exist and the greatest training school for men in this nation will have been destroyed." "Let us get away from this silly, female mushiness," wrote another alumnus to the *Richmond Evening Journal*. And the *Montgomery Messenger* of Christiansburg, Virginia, saw fit to declare that "there is no special need for highly educated women; until the nineteenth century men have always taken care of women; they can continue to do it in an improved way." What more should a woman want? She already had, said the *Montgomery Messenger*, "all she needs to make herself agreeable to men."[12]

Against that sort of obscurantism and complacency, educational leaders in Virginia and many other citizens joined the campaign for a Co-ordinate College which Mrs. Munford led. The struggle to achieve it became the most exciting fact in succeeding sessions of the Legislature. Crowds attended the hearings conducted by the Committees of the Senate and the House of Delegates, and filled the galleries of the two houses when the issue was brought to a vote. In 1914, for the first time a bill to create the college passed the Senate, but it was defeated in the House of Delegates.

Advocacy of the college was so eager and the opposition to it so unyielding that the atmosphere was full of electric tension. There were days when the cloud of debate was like a gathering storm from which it seemed that at any moment angry lightning might break through. But as happens in such matters, there was the occasional happy accident of speech which came like a sudden shaft of sunshine. One of the advocates of the college was a superb old lady who moved like a full-rigged ship, Mrs. Norman Randolph, who could and would speak her mind in no uncertain fashion, and whose impeccable devotion to Virginia traditions and to the United Daughters of the Confederacy, of whom she was the president, made even reluctant legislators listen with healthy respect when she added to her old interests an emphatic championship of the new cause of the Co-ordinate College. At one of the legislative hearings, the plan for the college had been denounced by a prominent lawyer, Mr. Eppa Hunton, who had been a childhood playmate and lifelong friend of Mrs. Randolph's. Mr. Hunton, who had married late, had a son who was about the age of Mrs. Randolph's grandchildren. In a speech preceding

Mrs. Randolph's arising, Mr. Hunton had pictured graphically the demoralization which he believed would come to the University of Virginia by the admission of women students to any connection there. He had pleaded his own love for the university and his supreme desire that his only son should go there, and declared that if the Co-ordinate College bill were passed his dearest hope would be destroyed because he would never be willing to send his son to the University of Virginia then. Mrs. Randolph took indignant note of this, and when she had finished the main part of her own speech to her satisfaction, she turned toward Mr. Hunton in a mood in which were mingled her old-time intimacy and the immediate fire of her ruffled spirit. "Eppie Hunton," she said, "you stood here a few minutes ago and said that if girls went to the University of Virginia it would spoil the University, and your little son, your darling son, could never go there. The girls of Virginia have just as much right to go to the University as the boys have; and don't you dare to stand there, Eppie Hunton, and tell me that the University would not be fit for your son to go to if my granddaughters should go there!" The galleries rocked with delighted amusement; and Mr. Hunton, in spite of his discomfiture, remembered to make Mrs. Randolph a profound, if very formal bow.

When the bill had been defeated in 1914, Mrs. Randolph wrote to Mrs. Munford:

> My dear child:
> For such you are to the old woman now writing you. I just felt I must send in writing my congratulations on your splendid fight against such heavy odds, with everything against you but your *splendid cause*. Defeated? not one bit of it! . . . Rally your forces in time for another attack. If you have the *Century* magazine of November 1891, article by Wilbur Fisk Tillett, Vanderbilt University, Nashville, read it and see if you are not the Joan of Arc that is to lead to

victory this women's movement for higher education. If I can be of any service to you, call on me. I can only add by my age, which has given me experience, to your efforts for the good of the women of Virginia.[13]

Mrs. Munford and her companions did come back to the Legislature of 1916. Again the bill to establish the college cleared the Committees of the two houses, and passed in the Senate by a decisive vote. It went over to the House of Delegates, and late in the session, after six hours of debate, the voting began. The gallery of the House of Delegates and the spaces on the floor behind the members' seats were jammed, and many people, unable to get into the chamber, watched from the corridor through the glass doors.

Down the list the voting went, the lead swinging by a very slight margin now this way and now that. When the roll call was finished, there was silence. Many people who had listened breathlessly were checking up their own notes. The clerk was slowly counting up his official record. He turned to the speaker. "The vote," he said "is forty-six, Aye; forty-eight, Nay." The bill was lost again.

That was in 1916. In 1917, the United States entered the First World War. When the Legislature met in 1918, engrossment with the war crowded out the question of the college. In its failure to give its women educational opportunities comparable to those it had given to men, the state of Virginia had let itself be content with what President Alderman had dreaded, "restricted effort and restricted ambition."

For Mary-Cooke Munford this long fight had come to its end. But she did not flag in her readiness to serve any cause that could help the disadvantaged. She continued to pour her energies into the work of the Co-operative Education Association. She became the first woman member of the School Board of the city of Richmond, a member of the Board of the College of William and Mary, and later of the Board of Visitors of the University of Virginia. At public hearings of the Richmond City Council she pleaded for the Negro people, whose needs too often were treated with indifferent concern. What her championship meant was indicated in a letter written to her by the pastor of one of the Richmond Negro churches:

> My only apology for addressing you these brief lines is an ardent desire to tell you how very grateful we are to you for the humane and courageous efforts which you are putting forth for . . . a people situated as we are, politically dead, and standing dumb at the bar of our city government. . . . For many years we have groaned in the prison of our uncomfortable and unsanitary surroundings, with bad streets and cramped and unsightly homes, praying for deliverance, and it may be that God ordains that you should open the eyes of our City Fathers, to see that even the black defenseless children of our municipality are deserving of some consideration in their working and planning for the welfare of the people of the City.[14]

Also, though the Co-ordinate College was never created, the long and gallant effort toward it was not without direct results for the girls of Virginia, whose need for larger opportunity had been so near to Mrs. Munford's heart. The ancient College of William and Mary was opened fully to women; and at the University of Virginia women at the graduate level were admitted, and the residence hall built for them was given Mary-Cooke Munford's name.

When she died, Douglas Southall Freeman, editor of the *Richmond News Leader,* wrote of her:

> If you would see her monument, look about you anywhere in the realm of Virginia education, of rural betterment, and of women's ampler life. Which of her many memorials is the greatest, who yet can say?

Perhaps it was the Co-operative Education Association, the burden of which she carried through discouraging years. Perhaps again her greatest monument was her own glowing, determined personality. In how many lives and for how long a time those great eyes of hers will shine!

In the library at the University of Virginia is this tablet:

MARY COOKE BRANCH MUNFORD
1865-1938

Member of the Board of Visitors
of this University
1926-1938

WHO CARRIED THE DEVOTION OF A
GREAT MIND AND A FLAMING SPIRIT
INTO UNSELFISH SERVICE TO PUBLIC
EDUCATION THROUGHOUT VIRGINIA

HER MEMORIAL IS IN NUMBERLESS
YOUNG LIVES SET FREE

❦ XI ❧

Helen Keller and Anne Sullivan Macy

These two names in the title of this chapter belong together, for Helen Keller was like a spirit shut in prison, and Anne Sullivan (afterward Mrs. Macy) was the person who set her free.

In Tuscumbia, a small town in northern Alabama, the little daughter of Arthur H. Keller, who had been a captain in the Confederate army, and of Kate Adams, his second wife, was a bright and happy child nineteen months old. Born on June 27, 1880, and named Helen, she had experienced, and registered in remembrance as far as a child's senses can, the sights and sounds of her world through a year and a half of infancy. Then came an illness—called by the country doctor "congestion of the stomach and the brain"—so acute that it was believed she could not live. She did recover, and there was great rejoicing. But then came the shattering discovery that she was both completely deaf and completely blind. And since she was too young to have learned language, she was cut off from all three chief roads of communication with people and things around her. She could not hear or see, and there were no words that she knew how to say.

Her father and mother surrounded her with affection. A little Negro girl named Martha Washington was her constant companion and responded with a child's readiness to her crude signs when they played together. But what about Helen herself? Back of the wall of blindness and deafness that shut her away from communication with other people, was any real mind working; or had her intelligence been destroyed along with her eyesight and her hearing? Was she only "a phantom living in a world that was no world"? No one could be sure, and meanwhile she was becoming increasingly unmanageable. She would express her desires for this or that by impulsive gestures, but when these gestures were not understood and answered her frustration would break out in furious resentment. Nevertheless, in their tenderness for the little crippled child, her father and mother could not bear to discipline her. What hope could the future hold?

One day Mrs. Keller happened to be reading in Charles Dickens' *American Notes,* and came upon Dickens' mention of the Perkins Institution for the Blind in Boston, and of how Dr. Samuel Gridley Howe had taught Laura Bridgman who, like Helen, was deaf and blind. Little by little he had reached her understanding, first by "pasting upon several common articles such as keys, spoons, knives, etc., little paper labels with the names of the articles printed in raised letters, which he got her to feel and differentiate; then he gave her the same labels by themselves, which she learnt to associate with the articles they referred to, until, with the spoon or knife alone before her she could find the right label for each from a mixed heap. The next stage was to give her the component letters and teach her to combine them in the words she knew; and gradually in this way she learnt all the alphabet and the ten digits." Also, by pressure of finger signs on the palm of her hand, he taught her the finger alphabet through which the names of things and ultimately ideas could be spelled out directly to her comprehension. "The whole process depended, of course, on her having a human intelligence, which only required stimulation. . . ."[1]

How could Helen find that sort of stimulation? It had been nearly fifty years since Dr. Howe had taught Laura Bridgman, and Dr. Howe was dead. But the Kellers took Helen to Baltimore to consult a famous oculist; and although he told them that Helen would never see or hear, he advised them to go to

Washington to talk with the great scientist, Alexander Graham Bell. Dr. Bell told them to write to Michael Anagnos, who had become head of the Perkins Institution in succession to Dr. Howe—to find out whether Mr. Anagnos thought that there might be anyone who could do for Helen what Dr. Howe had done for Laura Bridgman.

As a result of that inquiry, there was to enter into Helen Keller's life the teacher and friend who would be the inspiration for what would come to seem the miracle of her release.

Annie Sullivan was the daughter of Irish immigrants, born in the midst of squalid poverty. When she was eight years old her mother died, and her father disappeared. With a younger brother, she was put in the almshouse at Tewksbury, Massachusetts. She was half-blind, but nobody paid any attention to that in the next four years. Then when conditions in the almshouse had become so notorious in their degradation that an investigation was ordered, the twelve-year-old child rushed up to one of the members of the investigating committee and cried out, "I want to go to school!"

She was taken to the Perkins Institution for the Blind, and stayed there six years. Operations on both her eyes improved her vision enough for her to be able to read for brief periods, but always at some hazard. She mastered the manual alphabet so that she might communicate with the deaf. Graduating from the Perkins Institution in 1886, she had to find a way to make a living. Then came the Kellers' letter to Michael Anagnos. He thought of Annie Sullivan. Perhaps she could bring some of Dr. Howe's methods to the help of the blind-deaf child in Alabama. At any rate, she could try.

To all likelihood it seemed a forlorn attempt. A young woman who had not reached her twenty-first birthday, whose childhood had been bleak and bitter, who had had no education except six years in the school for the blind—how could she be equal to a task which had been accomplished only once before in history, and then by a great man, learned and experienced: bringing back into living contact with the world a child who could neither see nor hear? Nevertheless, that was the lonely venture which Anne Sullivan faced. It would have been hopeless if there had not been in this daughter of poverty that inexplicable richness of the human spirit which sometimes grows up out of the most barren ground: an imagination which could cope with the seemingly impossible, and a devotion which grew the more resolute when difficulties and discouragements increased.

It was on March 3, 1887, that Anne Sullivan arrived in Tuscumbia.

I found Mrs. Keller and Mr. James Keller [Helen's half-brother] waiting for me [she wrote to a friend]. They said somebody had met every train for two days. The drive from the station to the house, a distance of one mile, was very lovely and restful. . . . Captain Keller met us in the yard. . . . My first question was, "Where is Helen?" . . . As we approached the house I saw a child standing in the doorway, and Captain Keller said, "There she is. She has known all day that someone was expected, and she has been wild ever since her mother went to the station for you." I had scarcely put my foot on the steps, when she rushed toward me with such force that she would have thrown me backward if Captain Keller had not been behind me. She felt my face and dress and my bag, which she took out of my hand and tried to open. It did not open easily, and she felt carefully to see if there was a keyhole. Finding that there was, she turned to me, making the sign of turning a key and pointing to the bag. Her mother interfered at this point and showed Helen by signs that she must not touch the bag. Her face flushed, and when her mother attempted to take the bag from her, she grew very angry. . . . Somehow I had expected to see a pale, delicate child. . . . But there's nothing pale or delicate about Helen. She is large, strong, and ruddy, and as unrestrained in her movements as a young colt. . . . She rarely smiles;

indeed, I have seen her smile only once or twice since
I came. She is unresponsive and even impatient of
caresses from anyone except her mother. She is very
quick-tempered and wilful, and nobody, except her
brother James, has attempted to control her. The
greatest problem I shall have to solve is how to discipline and control her without breaking her spirit.
I shall go rather slowly at first and try to win her
love.[2]

But to win her love was not to be quick or easy, and was
only a part of a complex matter. Miss Sullivan was there not
just to please Helen by pandering to all her unrestrained
desires. She was there to reach this child's bewildered and
baffled spirit, and to help her toward self-knowledge and self-
control. In order to do that she had to teach her obedience.
That could be a painful business, but it had to be carried
through, nevertheless. It began in the first hours after Miss
Sullivan's arrival, and in those same hours began the development of the process by which the child could be made to
understand.

As Helen with "her untaught, unsatisfied hands" was pulling things out of the trunk which Miss Sullivan unpacked, she
found to her delight a doll which had been sent her by the
children at the Perkins Institution: "I thought it a good opportunity," Miss Sullivan wrote to a friend, "to teach her her
first word." So she spelled "d-o-l-l" slowly into Helen's hand
as she gave her the doll. "Spelled" it? one might ask. How
could there be any spelling for the child who had no language
and no letters? In the beginning there was, of course, no comprehension of what the particular touch of Miss Sullivan's
fingers meant. But an association was established. When Miss
Sullivan repeated the letters "d-o-l-l" as Helen held the doll,
she had the child imitate with her fingers the movements Miss
Sullivan's fingers had made. A little while afterward she went
downstairs and brought Helen a piece of cake, of which she
was very fond. "I showed Helen the cake," Miss Sullivan

wrote, "and spelled 'c-a-k-e' in her hand, holding the cake to-ward her. Of course, she wanted it and tried to take it; but I spelled the word again and patted her hand. She made the letters rapidly, and I gave her the cake, which she ate in a great hurry, thinking, I suppose, that I might take it from her. Then I showed her the doll, and spelled the word again, hold-ing the doll toward her as I had held the cake. She made the letters 'd-o-l' and I made the other 'l' and gave her the doll. She ran downstairs with it and could not be induced to return to my room all day."[3]

The next day Miss Sullivan gave her a sewing card with holes punched for worsted, on which Helen began to work delightedly. Then the teacher thought she would try another word, so she spelled into Helen's hand "c-a-r-d." Then she had Helen imitate the motions of her fingers. "She made the 'c-a,' then stopped and thought, and making the sign for eating and pointing downward she pushed me toward the door, meaning that I must go downstairs for some cake. The two letters 'c-a,' you see, had reminded her of Friday's 'lesson'—not that she had any idea that *cake* was the name of the thing, but it was simply a matter of association, I suppose."[4] She finished spell-ing the word "c-a-k-e" with Helen, and then went and brought cake to her, to the little girl's immediate satisfaction.

Thus there began to be glimmers of understanding, but not yet either obedience or love. Helen's table manners were ap-palling. In the dining room she would put her hands into every-body's plate and help herself, or snatch first at what was in the dishes when they were passed. When Miss Sullivan corrected this, Helen flung herself on the floor, kicking and screaming, and tried to jerk Miss Sullivan's chair from under her. It was an hour before Miss Sullivan could get the child in any way subdued; and this incident of furious resistance was only one of many. She had been so accustomed to behaving as she chose that she could not be coaxed or persuaded once her temper had been aroused. And when she was disciplined, the family were likely to interfere, especially her father, who could not bear to hear her cry.

Miss Sullivan concluded that she could not accomplish any-thing except in different surroundings. "I have thought about it a great deal," she wrote in one of her letters, "and the more I think, the more certain I am that obedience is the gateway through which knowledge, yes, and love too, enter the mind of the child."[5] So she told Captain and Mrs. Keller that Helen ought to be separated from the family for a few weeks at least. After a while they consented; and Miss Sullivan and Helen were installed in a little garden-house some distance from the main house, from which their meals were brought to them while the family kept away.

Helen was greatly excited at first, and kicked and screamed until she was almost in a stupor. She would not let Miss Sulli-van touch her. That night after she had played alone with her dolls she crept into the big double bed, but when she felt Miss Sullivan get into bed with her she leaped out on the other side. It took two hours for Miss Sullivan to get her into bed again, and she lay as near the edge as she could. The next morning she was quiet, but obviously homesick. She kept going to the door and touching her cheek, which was her sign for wanting her mother. She played with her dolls in an inter-mittent way, but she would have nothing to do with Miss Sullivan.

It was on March 3 that Miss Sullivan had arrived at Tuscumbia, and a week later that she and Helen went to the garden-house. Emotionally, it had been a stormy time. But on March 20, Miss Sullivan could write:

My heart is singing for joy this morning. A miracle has happened! The light of understanding has shone upon my little pupil's mind, and behold, all things are changed!

The wild little creature of two weeks ago has been transformed into a gentle child. She is sitting by me as I write, her face serene and happy, crocheting a long red chain of Scotch wool. She learned the stitch this week, and is very proud of the achievement. When she succeeded in making a chain that would reach across the room, she patted herself on the arm and put the first work of her hands lovingly against her cheek. She lets me kiss her now, and when she is in a particularly gentle mood, she will sit in my lap for a minute or two; but she does not return my caresses. . . . The little savage has learned her first lesson in obedience, and finds the yoke easy. It now remains my pleasant task to direct and mould the beautiful intelligence that is beginning to stir in the child-soul.[6]

Helen Keller's autobiography, and the letters of Miss Sullivan which are included in it, carry on the absorbing story of how the child's innate intelligence was led toward specific understanding, and given means of communication that would bypass the barriers of her blindness and her deafness. At first the child had only the vague awareness that the finger signs which her teacher made upon her palm had some sort of connection with things she wanted. Then on April 5, a month and two days after Miss Sullivan had come to the Keller family, she could record: "Helen has taken the second great step in her education. She has learned that *everything has a name, and that the manual alphabet is the key to everything she wants to know*."[7] That morning, when Helen was washing, Miss Sullivan had spelled "w-a-t-e-r" into her hand, but the child had not taken special notice. Later, Miss Sullivan took Helen out to the pump house, and this—in her words—is what followed:

. . . I made Helen hold her mug under the spout while I pumped. As the cold water gushed forth, filling the mug, I spelled "w-a-t-e-r" in Helen's free hand. The word coming so close upon the sensation of cold water rushing over her hand seemed to startle her. She dropped the mug and stood as one transfixed. A new light came into her face. She spelled "water" several times. Then she dropped on the ground and asked for its name and pointed to the pump and the trellis, and suddenly turning round she asked for my name.

In a postscript to the letter in which she had told about the water, Miss Sullivan added this:

> Helen got up this morning like a radiant fairy. She has flitted from object to object, asking the name of everything and kissing me for very gladness. Last night when I got in bed, she stole into my arms of her own accord and kissed me for the first time, and I thought my heart would burst, so full was it of joy.[8]

Little by little Miss Sullivan taught the child not only nouns as names of concrete things she could touch and feel, but also verbs, beginning with the simplest, such as *go* and *come*, and *eat* and *drink;* then adverbs and adjectives, such as *quickly* and *slowly*, and *soft* and *hard*. "It is wonderful," the happy teacher wrote, "how words generate ideas! Every new word Helen learns seems to carry with it necessity for many more. Her mind grows through its ceaseless activity."[9] Then Helen learned to write by pressing her pencil over a word-card on which the letters of the alphabet were stamped. Later she learned braille, and also how to use a typewriter.

In May of 1888 Helen was taken to Boston, where she made friends with the blind children at the Perkins Institution from which Miss Sullivan had come; and they spent that summer in New England. They came back to Alabama in the fall. In 1894, when Helen was fourteen, she was entered in the Wright-Humason School for the Deaf, in New York City, with Miss Sullivan still as her beloved and indispensable companion; and in 1896 she went to another school, in Cambridge, to achieve what had become her consummate ambition—to be admitted to Radcliffe College. Some of her friends thought that such an attempt went beyond the bounds of good sense—and let her know they thought so. How could she with her heavy handicaps meet the exactions of a college course? But she was determined to try. With the preparation which she got in school and with private tutoring, she passed the preliminary and final entrance examinations, and in the fall of 1900 she was enrolled in Radcliffe College—the same year, incidentally, in which Franklin D. Roosevelt entered Harvard.

"A potent force within me," she was to write in her auto-biography, "stronger than the persuasion of my friends, stronger even than the pleadings of my heart, had impelled me to try my strength by the standards of those who see and hear. I knew that there were obstacles in the way, but I was eager to overcome them."[10] She was not wrong about the obstacles. She could hear nothing in the lecture halls. Neither could she see the symbols and diagrams on the blackboards. Everything had to come to her through what Miss Sullivan listened to in lectures by her side or read in books and transmitted through her fingers. To surmount those obstacles did take—as generously admiring William Allan Neilson expressed it—"a courage and tenacity of purpose well-nigh appalling—the courage and the tenacity to face and to persist in the endless drudgery of learning, in spite of failure and discouragement and distrust, without the vision of the printed book or the sound of the teaching voice."[11]

In her separation from the other Radcliffe girls, it was true, as Helen Keller knew, that she must climb the Hill Difficulty alone. But in another sense, as she most deeply knew, she was not alone. What she was trying to do was undergirded and made possible by the self-forgetful devotion of Anne Sullivan, who at the hazard—and ultimately the destruction—of her own dim eyesight read for Helen Keller the books she could not read herself. No wonder the girl who knew so acutely her own limitations could exclaim: "My teacher is so dear to me that I can scarcely think of myself apart from her. . . . All the best of me belongs to her—there is not a talent, or an inspiration, or a joy in me that has not been awakened by her loving touch."[12]

In 1904 Helen Keller graduated from Radcliffe *cum laude*. The thrill of expectation with which she had entered college had been dimmed sometimes under the dull pressure of academic routine. She had begun her studies with eagerness because she thought she saw before her "a new world opening in beauty and light, . . . The lecture-halls seemed filled with the spirit of the great and the wise, and I thought the professors were the embodiment of wisdom." But after a time, the heavy succession of things that had to be done: reading assignments in disconnected subjects, term papers, examinations, made her begin to feel that there was "no time to commune with one's thoughts. One goes to college to learn, it seems, not to think. . . . It is impossible, I think, to read in one day four or five different books in different languages and treating of widely different subjects, and not lose sight of the very ends for which one reads. When one reads hurriedly and nervously, having in mind written tests and examinations, one's brain becomes encumbered with a lot of choice bric-à-brac for which there seems to be little use. . . . I do not mean to object to a thorough knowledge of the famous works we read. I object only to the interminable comments and bewildering criticisms that teach but one thing: that there are as many opinions as there are men."[13]

Thus she could feel in her harried moments; but all the same, she did come under the spell of teachers who inspired her: Charles Townsend Copeland in English composition, William James and Josiah Royce in philosophy, George Lyman Kittredge in English literature and especially in Shakespeare, where it was "as if new sight were given to the blind." When she had finished her course at Radcliffe she had learned much, and she had proved that in her quest for knowledge she could go on gallantly to the end of the road, not outstripped by those who being free from her limitations did not have to travel by her rough and tortuous way.

By the time she graduated from college, and even earlier, great numbers of people had begun to hear of Helen Keller. Articles about her had been published in *St. Nicholas* and the

Youth's Companion, two magazines which at the turn of the
century were widely and eagerly read. While she was in
Radcliffe, she had written *The Story of My Life,* which was to
have an immense circulation. Sometimes the curiosity about her,
and the exaggerations which some sensational writers indulged
in, were exasperating, especially to Anne Sullivan. But at the
basis of the public interest there was an emotion both instinctive and beautiful. Here was the story of a life that had broken
the dark spell which at first seemed to bind it. What had
happened between Helen Keller and her teacher was like a
fairy tale: a new fairy tale as of a Sleeping Beauty waked by a
kiss from sleep and silence to wondering recognition of the
world that belonged to her.

The amazing thing was the wideness of the world that did
become hers. The admiring interest which reached out to her
and the grateful warmth of her response brought her a circle
of friends such as few persons could have had. They included
some of the most distinguished persons in America: Alexander
Graham Bell, Phillips Brooks, Laurence Hutton, Edward
Everett Hale, Bishop David H. Greer, Senator George F. Hoar,
Oliver Wendell Holmes, Joseph Jefferson, William James,
William Dean Howells, Charles Dudley Warner, Mark Twain.
Instead of pitying herself for what she did not have, she
recognized the richness of what she did have. In what was perhaps her most remarkable book, *The World I Live In,* she revealed how, with sight and hearing gone, she still had gained
astonishing largeness of perception by developing, as most
people to any comparable degree seldom do, the three limited
senses she possessed: taste and smell and touch, especially touch.
This is the way she described what had become true for her:

> Ideas make the world we live in, and impressions
> furnish ideas. My world is built of touch-sensations,
> devoid of physical colour and sound; yet without
> colour and sound it breathes and throbs with life.
> Every object is associated in my mind with tactual
> qualities which, combined in countless ways, give me a

sense of power, of beauty, or of incongruity; for with
my hands I can feel the comic as well as the beautiful
in the outward appearance of things. . . . Necessity
gives to the eye a precious power of seeing, and in the
same way it gives a precious power of feeling to the
whole body. Sometimes it seems as if the very substance of my flesh were so many eyes looking out at
will upon a world new created every day. The silence
and darkness which are said to shut me in, open my
door most hospitably to countless sensations that dis-
tract, inform, admonish, and amuse. With my three
trusty guides, touch, smell, and taste, I make many
excursions into the borderland of experience which is
in sight of the city of Light. . . . It is not for me to say
whether we see best with the hand or the eye. I only
know that the world I see with my fingers is alive,
ruddy, and satisfying. Touch brings the blind many
sweet certainties which our more fortunate fellows
miss, because their sense of touch is uncultivated.
When they look at things, they put their hands in
their pockets.[14]

She could tell what individuals might be coming toward her
—child or adult, man or woman, young or old—by the different vibrations of footsteps on the floor. Also, she had her
sensitive way not only of knowing that someone was in her
presence, but of discerning almost instantly what sort of
person that someone was. "It is interesting," she wrote, "to
observe the differences in the hands of people. . . . Some hands,
when they clasp yours, beam and bubble over with gladness.
. . . Other people shake hands with me as if with the fear that I
may do them mischief. Such persons hold out civil finger-tips
which they permit you to touch, and in the moment of contact
they retreat, and inwardly you hope that you will not be called
upon again to take that hand of 'dormouse valour.' . . . But a
loving hand I never forget. I remember in my fingers the large

hands of Bishop Brooks, brimful of tenderness and a strong man's joy. If you were deaf and blind, and could have held Mr. [Joseph] Jefferson's hand, you would have seen in it a face and heard a kind voice unlike any other you have known."[15]

Moreover for her there was a special gateway to awareness through the sense of smell, which too often may be "neglected and disparaged." It is not only that she drew in, more acutely and rejoicingly than most people do, the rich odours of the outdoors: of flowers in the garden, apple blossoms unfolding in the spring, the dampness of plowed ground, salt air blowing off the sea. Also she could say:

> From exhalations I learn much about people. I often know the work they are engaged in. The odours of wood, iron, paint, and drugs cling to the garments of those that work in them. Thus I can distinguish the carpenter from the iron-worker, the artist from the mason or the chemist. When a person passes quickly from one place to another I get a scent impression of where he has been—the kitchen, the garden, or the sick-room. I gain pleasurable ideas of freshness and good taste from the odours of soap, toilet water, clean garments, woolen and silk stuffs, and gloves. . . . The dear odours of those I love are so definite, so unmistakable, that nothing can quite obliterate them. . . . Once, long ago, in a crowded railway station, a lady kissed me as she hurried by. I had not touched even her dress. But she left a scent with her kiss which gave me a glimpse of her. The years are many since she kissed me. Yet her odour is fresh in my memory.[16]

Thus Helen Keller, grievous though her limitations were, was no crippled personality. On the contrary, her spirit expanded to take possession of life in all ways that were possible to her. "The only lightless dark," she wrote, "is the light of ignorance and insensibility." Blindness and deafness could not take away from her "the things that count—service, friendship, humour, imagination, wisdom. It is the secret inner will that controls one's fate. We are capable of willing to be good, of loving and being loved, of thinking to the end that we may be wiser."[17]

When Helen Keller was a little girl she had made a struggling effort to learn to talk. Her vocal cords and her larynx were like those of any normal child, but intelligible speech had been impossible because she did not know the sound that letters or words were supposed to have, and could not distinguish those sounds if her vocal cords should manage to make them. But by putting her fingers on Miss Sullivan's throat and on her lips she tried to imitate what Miss Sullivan was saying, and she did succeed in making a few sounds near enough to words to be understood. Later, in New England, a vocal teacher, with immense generosity of time and patience, coached and trained her so that she got to the point of actually trying to speak in public. Guttural and strange though her speaking was, and attended at first with bitter discouragement and humiliation, it nevertheless was to its degree a triumph, and it would become vastly important in the work she was to do.

Not long after Helen had graduated from college, Miss Sullivan was married to John Albert Macy, a distinguished literary critic, whose friendship and advice helped Helen to produce *The Story of My Life*. All sunny prospects seemed to be opening for Anne Sullivan in her marriage; and for Helen in her companionship with both the Macys when she lived with them in Wrentham, Massachusetts. But unhappily, the marriage did not last, and Anne Sullivan Macy and Helen Keller were left alone again to go their way together. Besides what her father had been able to do for her in her girlhood, Helen had been generously helped toward her education by large-hearted men of wealth who had heard the gallant story of her life—particularly H. H. Rogers and Andrew Carnegie.

Nevertheless, financial problems beset them, and one way in which they tried to meet these was by engagements on the Orpheum Circuit, in which—sandwiched in between other specialties—Anne Macy would describe the process of Helen Keller's liberation, and Helen herself would speak as best she could about what could be done for the blind and deaf.

Eventually, happier avenues were to open—though more for Helen Keller than for her teacher, for Anne Macy's defective eyesight, which she had never spared in the years when she had had to be Helen's eyes, turned into almost total blindness, her general health weakened, and in 1936 she died. It was a shattering grief for Helen Keller; but, as she wrote in her book called *Teacher*, "There was such virtue and such power of communication in Teacher's personality that after her death they nerved me to endure and persevere. I was gripped by the might of the destiny she had mapped out for me, it lifted me out of myself to wage God's war against darkness."[18] There had been established the American Foundation for the Blind, and the American Foundation for Overseas Blind; and Miss Keller—companioned now by Miss Polly Thomson, of Glasgow, Scotland, who had come as secretary into the Macy-Keller household before Anne Macy's death—was enlisted to go to every one of the five continents and to nearly all the nations, carrying to government officials, to legislative committees, to public meetings and to private citizens, the plea of the blind in every country for understanding and for help.

Mark Twain had once said to her: "Helen, the world is full of unseeing eyes, vacant, staring, soulless eyes."[19] Always there is danger that the prosperous and contented may go about their complacent business, indifferent to the human tragedies around them. Helen Keller, lending her name and giving her devotion to organizations everywhere that serve the blind, has waked the consciences of many to see the needs that they may help to meet. Thus she whose life at first seemed shut in darkness has been the carrier of light.

❧ XII ❧

Eleanor Roosevelt

In New York of the 1880's a young matron who belonged to New York Society in that period when the word was written with a capital S, pouring tea in her drawing-room for an afternoon caller, looked up to see a hesitant child standing in the doorway. "Come in, Granny," she said; and then, aside to the visitor, "She is such a funny child, so old-fashioned that we always call her 'Granny.'"

The lady who spoke was Mrs. Elliott Roosevelt; the little girl, her daughter, was Eleanor Roosevelt.

"My mother," the child was to write years afterward, "belonged to that New York City Society which thought itself all-important. Old Mr. Peter Marié, who gave choice parties and whose approval stamped young girls and young matrons a success, called my mother a queen, and bowed before her charm and beauty, and to her this was important."[1]

The little daughter was quite different. She was not beautiful, and she knew it painfully. She was awkward and shy and solemn, and she seldom smiled. She had a child's hunger for affection and praise, and all the more wistfully because she was fully conscious of her plain looks and her awkward manners. "My mother was always a little troubled by my lack of beauty," she remembered, "and I knew it as a child senses such things. She tried very hard to bring me up well so my manners would in some way compensate for my looks, but her efforts only made me more keenly conscious of my shortcomings."[2]

The bright spot in her life was her father, for whom she had a little daughter's adoration. He was a brother of Theodore Roosevelt, and had much of the verve and overflowing zest for life which characterized that more famous member of the family. As a boy of fifteen, when he had had to leave St. Paul's School on account of illness, he had gone to Texas, where he made friends with the army officers at the frontier Fort McKavit, hunted wild turkeys and other game, and rode with scouting parties which patrolled a region where there still were bands of hostile Indians. After that he went around the world, and hunted big game in India. At his country house on Long Island he played polo, and had exuberant pleasure in his dogs and horses. But riding in a society circus, he broke his leg; and following that he began to drink. From that time on he became increasingly a problem for the family; and to the child's troubled and perplexed awareness there came a foreboding which was the worse because she could not understand it. She slept in her mother's room; and sometimes she would be awake when her mother, thinking she was asleep, might be talking at her own bedtime to some member of the family. "I acquired," she said, "a strange and garbled idea of the troubles which were going on around me. Something was wrong with my father, and from my point of view nothing could be wrong with him."[3]

When Eleanor was eight years old her mother died of diphtheria. Her father, who had been sent away because of his drinking, arrived too late for anything except bitter loneliness and despair—and the knowledge that his wife had wanted her mother, not her husband, to be the guardian of their children. Eleanor and her two brothers went to live with her grandmother who was a widow, Mrs. Hall. Only occasionally could her father come to see her, but he was still the center of her devotion. In 1894, when she was not quite ten years old, he died.

Life in her grandmother's Victorian brownstone house on West 37th Street in New York City was not a happy experience, although her two young aunts and two uncles were always good to her. So also in her intention was Grandmother Hall, but her ideas as to what a young girl should do and not do were exceedingly formal, and if the granddaughter asked permission for anything outside the usual routine the answer was generally "No," with no further reason given.

When Eleanor was fifteen, a new and different chapter in her life began. One of her mother's sisters, Mrs. Mortimer, was going to Europe, and it was decided that Eleanor should sail with her to England and be entered there in Allenswood School, near London, where one of her father's sisters, "Auntie Bye," had been a pupil a generation earlier. Mlle Souvestre, the head of the school, liked Eleanor Roosevelt as she came to know her. At the Easter holiday in the second year at school Mlle Souvestre invited Eleanor to travel with her to Italy, and to the girl whose movements had been controlled by Grandmother Hall's prearranged and unvarying patterns, traveling with Mlle Souvestre was a revelation. One day on a train bound for Pisa where their reservations had been made, toward evening the guard called out "Alassio." On an instant's impulse, Mlle Souvestre thrust her head out of the compartment window. "I am going to get off," she called; and with Eleanor snatching up their bags, the two of them fell off onto the station platform. "My friend Mrs. Humphrey Ward lives here," said Mlle Souvestre, when she had caught her breath, "and I decided that I would like to see her. Besides, the Mediterranean is a very lovely blue at night and the sky with the stars coming out is nice to watch from the beach."

As a matter of fact, it turned out that Mrs. Ward was away. The best hotel was crowded and they had to go to a second-rate one. All the same, they spent the evening on the beach looking at the sea and the sky, and although seventy-year-old Mlle Souvestre had a cold the next day she was not in the least regretful. "And I had learned a valuable lesson," Eleanor Roosevelt wrote in her recollections. "Never again would I be the rigid little person I had been theretofore."[4]

Three years at Allenswood came to an end. Eleanor had

liked the school and all its associations; and in the holidays she had been again to Italy, to Switzerland, Germany, and Belgium, to Paris and to southern France, and to the Passion Play at Oberammergau. The inhibited girl who had come first to England had a new range of interests, and was beginning to discover herself.

Back at Grandmother Hall's, however, she must fit herself again into the proper conventions. Unquestionably, she must "come out." So her first winter at home was the round of dances, luncheons, teas, and dinners which constituted introduction into society. As to it all, she had a painfully divided mind. She was still conditioned by her upbringing, and believed that to be "a success" in New York society was a matter of acute importance. But a success was what she knew she was not likely to be. So it proved at her first Assembly Ball, which was "utter agony." With extraordinary directness of self-appraisal, she could admit what appeared at the time to be the humiliating fact: "There was absolutely nothing about me to attract anybody's attention. I was tall, but I did not dance very well. . . . I knew I was the first girl in my mother's family who was not a belle, and though I never acknowledged it to any of them at that time, I was deeply ashamed."[5] If the ultimate realities had depended upon the surface indications, it would not have seemed likely that Eleanor Roosevelt would emerge as a significant person.

But she was making friends in New York in circles of more consequence than the Assembly Ball. As a member of the newly formed Junior League, she undertook to teach a class of children at the Rivington Street Settlement House, and went there faithfully even though the evening walk along the Bowery filled her "with a certain amount of terror." On behalf of the Consumer's League, she went through factories and department stores to investigate the wages and the conditions of work—often abominable—of the women who made and sold the clothes which other women bought and wore. It was her first introduction to the stark contrast between the

world the girls of her set moved in, and the industrial world
in which other girls not born to her privileges had to earn
their livelihood. She was developing what was to became more
characteristic of her generation than of the comfortable generation preceding hers—a social conscience.

At the same time, she was finding interesting and stimulating
friends in New York, and in Washington where Theodore
Roosevelt, her "Uncle Ted," was in the White House. Also
she was gaining more self-possession. Conscious that she possessed a strong sense of duty, she wanted to do right; but how
could she be sure she was doing the right thing if someone criti-
cized her? Her beloved "Auntie Bye" put into her mind what
could become her answer to that question. "No matter what
you do," she said, "some people will criticize you, and, if
you are entirely sure that you would not be ashamed to explain
your action to someone whom you loved and who loved you,
and you are satisfied in your own mind that you are doing
right, then you need never worry about criticism, nor need
you ever explain what you do."[6]

About to graduate from Harvard at this time was Franklin
Delano Roosevelt, a fifth-cousin-once-removed. He fell in
love with Eleanor and asked her to marry him. In the autumn
of 1904 their engagement was announced, and in March 1905
they were married. The bride was given away by her "Uncle
Ted," and because as President of the United States he was to
come to New York to review a parade at that time, the date set
for the wedding was March 17th, St. Patrick's Day.

For the next quarter century Eleanor Roosevelt would live
in various places, as her husband's interests and responsibilities
widened: in New York, Albany, Hyde Park, Washington.
Ultimately, she would be so widely known as to be thought
of as a public figure, but her first concern was that of any
devoted young wife and mother: her own home and her family.
Six children were born, of whom one died in babyhood. "I
had always been a particularly healthy person," she wrote in
This Is My Story, "and I think it was a good thing for me

to be perfectly miserable for three months before every one of my six babies arrived, as it made me a little more understanding and sympathetic of the general illnesses human beings are subject to."⁷

In 1910 Franklin Roosevelt, who had graduated from the Columbia Law School after finishing at Harvard, and had been in a law office in New York City, ran for a Senate seat in the New York Legislature, and was elected. So it was in Albany that there began for Eleanor Roosevelt what she recognized as "a dual existence for me, which was to last all the rest of my life. Public service, whether my husband was in or out of office, was to be a part of our daily life from now on. . . . It was a wife's duty to be interested in whatever interested her husband, whether it was politics, books or a particular dish for dinner. This was the attitude with which I approached that first winter in Albany."⁸

In 1913 Woodrow Wilson, newly inaugurated as President of the United States, invited Franklin Roosevelt to Washington as Assistant Secretary of the Navy; and from then until 1920, Washington was to be the Roosevelts' home. It was characteristic of Eleanor Roosevelt that when any responsibility came to her she accepted it as something that had to be carried out completely. "I still lived under the compulsion of my early training. . . . I looked at everything from the point of view of what I ought to do, rarely from the standpoint of what I wanted to do."⁹ She did not like a continual round of official social calls, for she had always been shy; but as the wife of the Assistant Secretary of the Navy, she was supposed to make them, and every afternoon she did. Then in 1917 the United States became a combatant in the First World War, and for every person connected with official circles in Washington responsibilities became heavier and life more tense. This was immediately the fact for the Assistant Secretary of the Navy, and by consequence also for his wife. One way in which Eleanor Roosevelt could be directly helpful was by accompanying her husband on many of his strenuous trips of inspection to port cities and to naval installations, so she went. Some of these trips, with the inevitable mishaps of travel schedule, and with the well-meant but exhausting exactions of reception committees, made demands on bodily endurance that were almost intolerable; but Eleanor Roosevelt was learning from all this that she was capable of more than she had ever thought. She could say, "I never let anything physical prevent my doing whatever had to be done. . . . I think I knew instinctively, that these trips were just one of the tests that life puts in your way as a preparation for the future. They were feats of endurance, and, in the doing, they built up strength. I learned that I could be tired and that it did me no harm. Sometime or other I had to catch up on sleep, but I learned that if I kept myself well, when I had an exhausting strain to endure, it could be borne."[10]

"The tests that life puts in your way as a preparation for the future": these were to come to Eleanor Roosevelt in increasing measure, and the result was to intensify her conviction that they could be so met as to "build up strength." As often happens in human affairs, the kind of test which may come next and for which strength will be needed may be such as would have seemed least predictable.

When the administration of President Wilson drew toward its end and a national election was to be held in 1920, Franklin Roosevelt was nominated for Vice-President on the Democratic ticket, but the Democrats were defeated and Roosevelt was back in private life, resuming law practice in New York. In the summer vacations the family went to Campobello Island, off the coast of Maine, where in all outdoor life on land and sea Franklin Roosevelt was exultantly at home. One day in 1921 when he was out sailing he saw a forest fire, and he and the others who were with him went ashore to fight it. Coming home about four o'clock in the afternoon, hot from putting out the fire, he decided to go for a swim; and back from that, in his wet bathing suit he sat down to look at letters which the mail had brought. That evening he had a chill, and went to bed before supper. The next morning, fever; after that, something that seemed to be wrong with his legs; a visit from the local doctor, who was uncertain what was the matter; then the arrival of a specialist sent for at the persuasion of Frederic Delano, Franklin Roosevelt's uncle; and his verdict— infantile paralysis. Next came the complicated and painful business for Roosevelt of being carried on a stretcher off the rocky island, by a small motorboat across the two miles of rough water to the mainland, through the window into the compartment of a Pullman car; and so to New York to be taken, again on a stretcher, by ambulance to the Presbyterian Hospital. The handsome young man of superb vitality was now a cripple.

What would be his future? To his mother, Mrs. James Roosevelt, there seemed to be one certain answer. As her only son, he had always been the center of her brooding devotion. Now that he was ill, he must not tax himself any more with active responsibilities. He should come home to Hyde Park where he had been born and lived as a boy and grown to be a man, be taken care of, settle down to the carefree life of a country squire, get back his ability to walk if complete attention to that could make it possible, and in any case not do anything that would jeopardize his physical well-being further. With matriarchal intensity she brought her persuasion to bear, convinced in her own mind that any other decision for her son would be a cruel wrong.

For Eleanor Roosevelt, this was a crisis that taxed her to the uttermost. She could understand her mother-in-law's unbounded solicitude for her son; and all her own protectiveness as a woman and a wife could have been drawn in the same direction—toward the sheltered life which would make least demands on him. But that would put an end to his public usefulness. To let him retire to the placid shelter of Hyde Park might seem the compassionate solution for an invalid; but what did this mean except treating the whole man, and not just his legs, as though henceforth he had to be a cripple? Was it instead the brave thing and the right thing to believe that he himself was bigger than his limitations, and to keep him in the main stream of life, even at risk and hazard?

In the Roosevelt circle and as closely tied into it as though he had become a member of the family was the little gnome-like figure of Louis McHenry Howe. Since the time when Franklin Roosevelt had campaigned for the New York Senate and been elected to it, Louis Howe, a newspaper man with an almost uncanny prescience, had believed that Roosevelt could attain unlimited public eminence, and had devoted himself to mobilizing the influences which would make this come true. The infantile paralysis did not shake his intense conviction. Eleanor Roosevelt was moved by a belief which was not identical with Louis Howe's, but which ran parallel to it. She was not caught up in his passionate obsession with particular political objectives; but she recognized that Franklin Roosevelt had great capacities for public service, and that a part of his essential self would be sacrificed if he shut the door upon it. "Franklin needs rest and complete quiet," said his mother; and when Eleanor did not agree, Mrs. James Roosevelt turned one day to Louis Howe and said to him:

> "You have good common sense. Can't you see that a political future is now out of the question for my son? He always wanted to write, and when he comes home to Hyde Park he can keep busy doing that or reading books or collecting stamps."
>
> Louis Howe snapped at her, "I expect him to be President."
>
> Then, staring at Franklin, Howe said angrily, "Sure you can retire and become a country squire like your father, or you can take up where you left off and go right on. So far as I'm concerned you're a man of destiny."[11]

Whether or not she could believe then in Louis Howe's prediction of what Franklin might arrive at, Eleanor Roosevelt was determined to have him feel that the best of his life lay ahead of him and not behind him, and so with patient steadfastness she stood against her mother-in-law's effort to treat Franklin only as an invalid. She kept him in New York City, though she had to cope day and night with a crowded and complicated household situation which included the comings and goings of the children, her husband's nurses, and Louis Howe. At the same time, at Howe's persuasion, she was trying to identify herself more and more with outside interests and activities, for the express purpose of bringing the stimulus of these to her husband's thinking and making personal contacts which would be his also.

For a considerable time Franklin had acute and continual pain in his legs and back. Gradually the pain ceased, but his legs were withered. By the next spring, with a heavy brace on each leg and with crutches, he could stand erect. Because he had to use the upper part of his body so much to compensate for the paralyzed legs, his chest and arms developed great strength. But he would never move about again unaided. Louis Howe's stubborn insistence that unlimited possibilities of public service still opened before him would have seemed to most people to be nothing more than a foolish notion.

Nevertheless, out of what seemed disaster there did come astonishing gain. The suffering which Franklin Roosevelt had to undergo and the long and patient struggle he had to wage to overcome as far as he could the crippling which the paralysis had brought, bred in him an indomitable courage which would show itself in later years. "Once I spent two years lying in bed trying to move my big toe," he said long afterward to someone who was marveling at his ability to stand the particular strain which he then was under. "That was the hardest job I ever had to do. After that, anything else looked easy."[12] His wife recognized that the whole experience of his illness "gave him a strength and depth . . . [of character] . . . that he did not have as a young man."[13] And as a consequence of that same illness Eleanor Roosevelt was to be projected into new relationships which would have decisive effect in the unfolding within herself of possibilities then unforeseen. It was as though there had come true for both of them the prescient words which Ralph Waldo Emerson had written long before:

> . . . the compensations of calamity are made apparent to the understanding also, after long intervals of time. A fever, a mutilation, a cruel disappointment . . . seems at the moment unpaid loss and unpayable. But the sure years reveal the deep remedial force that underlies all facts. . . . [That] which seemed nothing but privation, somewhat later assumes the aspect of a guide or genius; for it commonly operates revolutions in our way of life, terminates an epoch of infancy or of youth which was waiting to be closed, breaks up a wonted occupation, or a household, or style of living, and allows the formation of new ones more friendly to the growth of character. It permits or constrains the formation of new acquaintances, and the reception of new influences, that prove of the first importance to the next years; and the man or woman who would have remained a sunny garden-flower, with no room for its roots and too much sunshine for its head, by the falling of the walls and the neglect of the gardener, is made the banian of the forest, yielding shade and fruit to wide neighborhoods of men.[14]

If Franklin Roosevelt's career in politics was to be enlarged, he had to be kept in contact during his illness with public facts. But how? Louis Howe gave one answer. "*You* are going into politics," he said to Eleanor Roosevelt. So at his urging she not only worked in the League of Women Voters as head of a committee to gather and report the current facts about Congress and the issues before it; she became associated also with the Women's Trade Union League and the Democratic State Committee. In the Women's Trade Union League she came to know Maude Schwartz and Rose Schneiderman, two women exceptionally well grounded in labor history and theory. "Bring them home to Franklin," commanded Louis Howe. Moreover, Howe insisted that Eleanor Roosevelt learn to make a speech in public, including writing one and repeating it to him a dozen times. In her awkward shyness, her voice would break into what sounded like a nervous laugh or a high-pitched giggle. "Why do you laugh when you're making a serious speech and there wasn't anything funny?" he demanded. "Don't do it again." Also, he told her, "Keep this in mind. Have something to say, say it and then sit down."[15]

In 1928, Alfred E. Smith was nominated by the Democratic party for President of the United States. Franklin Roosevelt was in Warm Springs, Georgia, trying by swimming in the pool there to bring back some aliveness into his crippled legs. With the hope of strengthening his chances of winning the presidential election by carrying New York State, Smith brought to bear all the pressure he could muster to persuade Roosevelt to run for Governor of New York. That meant a hard decision. Long periods at Warm Springs seemed to offer the only chance for Roosevelt to regain any measure of his lost mobility. How could he go through the arduousness of a political campaign without being physically worse? "I'm not well enough to run, and that's all there is to it," he said. He sent a telegram to Smith. "I must with great regret confirm my decision not to accept the nomination and I know you will understand." But Smith and his associates, by telegram and telephone, kept up their plea. They needed him. The Democratic Party needed him. Finally Roosevelt surrendered. He would run.

The result was fateful. Smith was heavily defeated for the presidency, but by a narrow majority Roosevelt was elected Governor of New York. Two years later he was re-elected. Now Louis Howe's ambition for him was at full tide. In 1932 what he had dared to prophesy came true. Franklin D. Roosevelt was elected President of the United States; and Eleanor Roosevelt, with him in the White House, had to face the new and complex responsibilities involved in being the President's wife.

The first thing she had to do was what naturally fell within a woman's province: to make the White House a home for her husband and all the family and a place which would have an atmosphere of warmth. The building itself—which fifteen years later was discovered to have so deteriorated that almost the whole interior had to be torn out and rebuilt—was already falling into serious disrepair, and in its kitchen and other working quarters was so out of date as to lower the morale of any human beings who had to work there. Mrs. Roosevelt had the whole kitchen modernized, and the formerly shabby basement rooms which were all that the help had had to rest in completely changed. One servant spoke for himself and others when he said, "Oh, Lord, I don't know what we would do here without Mrs. Roosevelt."[16]

At the same time she recognized that improving the domestic arrangements in the White House went only a little way toward making sure that it would not be for the President a sort of official prison. As Frances Perkins, Secretary of Labor, wrote in *The Roosevelt I Knew*, "A daily diet of politicians and government officers gets quite dreary. . . . Mrs. Roosevelt . . . made a point of bringing in, in an informal way, a great many people from all walks of life. Politicians, scholars, writers, churchmen, as well as personal friends . . . theater people, musicians, artists, scientists, and explorers. Thus the President's natural, varied interests were satisfied, and he was able to endure the relative confinement of his life with more ease and grace."[17]

Other women before had been in the position of mistress of the White House and had won the country's respect and sometimes its affection. But no one before had reached out to such largeness of public service or had attained a stature in the eyes not only of America but of the world as this new First Lady was destined to do. It was not that she sought publicity. It was not that she was seeking honor. Neither one attracted her. The simple fact was that her mind was not on Eleanor Roosevelt. It was on other people and other people's needs, wherever those needy people were.

Both as Governor of New York and then as President of the United States, Franklin Roosevelt had a concern for the disadvantaged. With the pressure of the inescapable and endless responsibilities that bound him to his desk in Albany and later in the White House, besides the steel braces that weighed upon his legs, he could not often go to see for himself aspects of the nation's life about which he needed to know. His wife became for him to an extraordinary degree his eyes and ears. Her help could begin with something so specific as inspection of public institutions. With his inability to walk, he could not go inside an institution and get a real idea of how it was being run from the point of view of overcrowding, staff, food, and medical care. Therefore, while he was Governor of New York, she was asked to take over this part of the inspection. "At first," she said, "my reports were highly unsatisfactory to him. I would tell him what was on the menu for the day and he would ask: 'Did you look to see whether the inmates actually were getting that food?' I learned to look into the cooking pots on the stove and to find out if the contents corresponded to the menu; I learned to notice whether the beds were too close together, and whether they were folded up and put in closets or behind doors during the day, which would indicate that they filled the corridors at night; I learned to watch the patients' attitude towards the staff; and before the end of our years in Albany, I had become a fairly expert reporter on state institutions."[18]

When she was in the White House, she continued to do on a wider scale for her husband, now the President, what she had done for him when he was Governor of New York. Her powers of observation had greatly grown; and when to these there was added her compassionate interest in human beings, she could bring back to him an immediate awareness of realities in American life which otherwise might have come to him only as impersonal statistics. What this could mean was exemplified in the first year of his presidency, when the country was in the deep trough of economic depression which the new administration had inherited. In some of the states, especially where there were many coal mines, which now were closed down, conditions were desperate. Eleanor Roosevelt went into West Virginia, invited by the relief committee of the Quakers. "My husband agreed that it would be a good thing to do," she wrote, "so the visit was arranged. I had not been photographed often enough then to be recognized, so I was able to spend a whole day going about the area near Morgantown, West Virginia, without anyone's discovering who I was."

Then her account continued:

The conditions I saw convinced me that with a little leadership there could develop in the mining areas, if not a people's revolution, at least a people's party, patterned after some of the previous parties born of bad economic conditions. There were men in that area who had been on relief for from three to five years and had almost forgotten what it was like to have a job at which they could work for more than one or two days a week. There were children who did not know what it was to sit down at a table and eat a proper meal.

One story which I brought home from that trip I recounted at the dinner table one night. In a company house I visited, where the people had evidently seen better days, the man showed me his weekly pay slips. A small amount had been deducted toward his bill at the company store and for his rent and for oil for his mine lamp. These deductions left him less than a dollar in cash each week. There were six children in the family, and they acted as though they were afraid of strangers. I noticed a bowl on the table filled with scraps, the kind that you or I might give to a dog, and I saw children, evidently looking for their noonday meal, take a handful out of that bowl and go out munching. That was all they had to eat.

As I went out, two of the childen had gathered enough courage to stand by the door, the little boy holding a white rabbit in his arms. It was evident that it was a most cherished pet. The little girl was thin and scrawny, and had a gleam in her eyes as she looked at her brother. She said, "He thinks we are not going to eat it, but we are," and at that the small boy fled down the road, clutching the rabbit closer than ever.

It happened that William C. Bullitt was at dinner that night and I have always been grateful to him for the check he sent me the next day, saying he hoped that it might help to keep the rabbit alive.[19]

Because of her firsthand knowledge of conditions which the President could not see with his own eyes, and because of her informed concern, Mrs. Roosevelt from time to time could interpret to the President appeals for action brought to him by public servants for adventures in human welfare which conventional politicians were afraid of. In the bleak financial and business depression of the early 1930's, thousands of young people were idle. Harry Hopkins and Aubrey Williams came to Eleanor Roosevelt with an urgent hope that a National Youth Administration be created, to carry on the Civilian Conservation Corps, and in other ways to give high school youngsters a chance for further training and for usefulness. They thought the idea might rouse fierce opposition from those whose tendency was to label any new government activity as "socialistic," and they were hesitant to ask the President to commit himself. Would she find out what his feelings were? She did talk with him, and she made clear the apprehension Hopkins and Williams had. "He looked at me and asked: 'Do you think it is right to do this?' I said they thought it might be a great help to the young people, but they did not want him to forget that it might be unwise politically. . . . Then Franklin said: 'If it is the right thing to do for the young people, then it should be done. I guess we can stand the criticism, and I doubt if our youth can be regimented in this way or in any other way.' "[20]

As a result, the National Youth Administration was created; and as a matter of fact, turned out to be popular. That would certainly not prove always to be true for Eleanor Roosevelt in regard to other causes which she espoused. She did her utmost to have some of the abominable slum conditions in Washington cleaned up, but she got more opposition than response. Other activities of hers that called attention to social ills which the complacent did not want to recognize made some people wish they could shut her up somewhere. There was point in the laughing remark of the President one day. Mrs. Roosevelt had gone off in the morning, before the President was awake, to visit a prison in Baltimore with the director of industries for convicts who wanted her to see the salvage work being done there. When the President, on his way to his office, asked where she was, one of the secretaries answered, "She's in prison, Mr. President." "I'm not surprised," said [he], "but what for?"[21]

In her eagerness to help any individual or group who seemed to her to be struggling for justice and larger opportunity, she sometimes went beyond the line of prudence and became involved in what she afterward was frank to admit had been mistakes. At a period when there was disillusionment and the possibility of great bitterness among the youth of the country in regard to conditions which seemed to deny them opportunity, she was approached by leaders of the American Youth Congress. "I believed, of course," she said, "that these young people had the right to be heard. They had the right to fight for the things they believed in as citizens of a democracy. It was essential to restore their faith in the power of democracy to meet their needs, or they would take the natural path of looking elsewhere."[22] It was asserted in some quarters that some of the members of the Congress were Communists. Mrs. Roosevelt had them come to the White House and she told them she must know the unquestionable truth. They answered that they had no connection with any Communist organization and no interest in Communist ideas. She accepted their word. When some of them were summoned before the so-called Committee on Un-American Activities of the U. S. House of Representatives, she went to be present at the hearing, because she had heard that when that Committee "had before them people of little influence and backing their questions were so hostile as to give the impression that the witness had been haled before a court and prejudged a criminal," and "if there is one thing I dislike it is intimidating people instead of trying to get at facts."[23] Later she discovered that although the young people who first sought her aid may have been completely honest, there was evidence that others might have begun to infiltrate the American Youth Congress with Communist ideas, and she broke all connection with the Congress. The whole incident made her the target for savage criticism from the comfortable and the satisfied who resented her disturbing activities in general. But she kept her poise; and her unshaken purpose in spite of risks, to stand by the unemployed, the poor and the oppressed, and any minorities that seemed to be unfairly dealt with. "It is useless to resent anything," she wrote. "One must learn to look on whatever happens as part of one's education." So it did not disturb her, and instead could wake amusement, when in election years many women who did not like the President or the policies he represented wore large campaign buttons which declared, "We don't want Eleanor either."[24]

When the Second World War began, and especially after the United States had entered it, Mrs. Roosevelt's activities outside the White House began to extend around the world. The President felt that it might help the morale of the men in the worst places of the war front if a visit from her could bring a sense of the personal concern which he himself could not leave Washington to express. It was not an easy or pleasant commission to accept. Eleanor Roosevelt knew that many men of the top brass might resent her coming: resent the presence in their area of a woman who had neither official status nor military training, who supposedly would take their time for silly ceremonial welcome, and then be in everybody's way as she went around asking meddlesome questions. As a matter of fact, this was exactly the mood she did meet on her first arrivals at bases overseas. But the notable fact was that men who had been hostile to her coming recognized in a short time the stimulus she brought. She did not ask or accept any special consideration. She traveled by whatever ordinary transport might be available; she lived under the same harsh conditions that the military personnel had to face. And she was tireless in her concern for the actual human beings who to her were not merely so many military units known apart by the different numbers on their dogtags. She went through the rest camps and hospitals in New Zealand and Australia; to Guadalcanal while it was still being bombed by the Japanese, to Christmas Island, Samoa, Fiji, New Caledonia, and a long succession of other areas of the war in the Pacific. Then later she went 13,000 miles around the Caribbean, including posts as distant and seemingly insignificant as the Galapagos Islands where men stationed in that region felt that they were in a useless backwater, but to whom the President wanted her to carry the message that they were not forgotten and that their necessary business of being on watch for submarines had the nation's honor. Here as elsewhere she took with her lists of names sent to her by countless mothers, wives, sweethearts, and sisters who begged her to see their menfolk. She did see them, and when she came home she wrote letters by the hundreds telling about the men she had seen and conveying the messages they sent by her.

Then, before the war was ended, came Franklin Roosevelt's death in Warm Springs, Georgia; the bringing his body back over the long miles where at little railroad stations and at country crossroads people stood through the night to see the train go by; the funeral service in the White House; the burial of his body in the rose garden at Hyde Park.

For Eleanor Roosevelt it was the end of an era and the beginning of another, the nature of which could not be foreseen. "I had to face the future," she realized, "as countless other women have faced it without their husbands. . . . I had few definite plans but there were certain things I did not want to do. I did not want to run an elaborate household again. I did not want to cease trying to be useful in some way. I did not want to feel old—and I seldom have."[25]

According to Franklin Roosevelt's desire, the big house at Hyde Park which had always been his home was given to the government, and when President Harry S. Truman accepted it in the name of the people, Eleanor Roosevelt expressed the hope that all who should come there might feel Franklin Roosevelt's spirit "in this house, in the library, and in the rose garden where he wished his grave to be."[26] For herself she had a smaller house not far away, and she rented an apartment in New York City. "As the time went on," she wrote afterward, "the fact that I kept myself well occupied made my loneliness less acute. I am not sure whether this was due to my own planning or simply to circumstances. But . . . if you have work to do and do it to the best of your ability you will not have much time to think about yourself."[27]

That she would have work to do and that she would be useful was to be abundantly evident in the succeeding years. The first important fact was that President Truman appointed her as a member of the United States delegation to the United Nations. When that appointment was broached to her she listened to it at first "in fear and trembling,"[28] for she doubted whether she had the experience and the special knowledge which that responsibility would require. But she believed the United Nations to be the best hope for a peaceful world, and she knew that her husband had placed great importance on its establishment. So she accepted the appointment; and having done so, she gave to the work her full dedication of time and energy. It soon became evident to the other members of the delegation that she could be depended upon not only for alert understanding of large issues, but also for unflagging thoroughness in what was often the exhausting business of mastering facts. She was made the United States representative on the Commission on Human Rights, and was elected chairman of it. When one of the crucial recommendations of that Commission was submitted to the General Assembly, the United States delegation chose Mrs. Roosevelt to present her country's position as against the Russian spokesman, Andrei Vishinsky. That night as she walked wearily up the steps of her hotel she heard behind her the voices of the two Republican members of the American delegation, Senator Arthur Vandenburg and John Foster Dulles. One of them said to her, "Mrs. Roosevelt, we must tell you that we did all we could to keep you off the United Nations delegation. We begged the President not to nominate you. But now we feel we must acknowledge that we have worked with you gladly and found you good to work with. And we will be happy to do so again."[29]

When the Truman term in office came to an end with the election to the presidency of Dwight D. Eisenhower, Mrs. Roosevelt submitted her resignation as a United Nations delegate. Freed now from official responsibility she was none the less devoted to the United Nations cause. She volunteered to work with the American Association for the United Nations, the purpose of which is to stimulate public support for what the United Nations is and does. Convinced that one of the crucial needs in the aim to preserve peace is a more sure and sympathetic knowledge of world conditions, she began to go to many countries: to see, to listen, and to learn; to find out the human facts, and try to interpret what she found. She went to Lebanon, Jordan, Israel, Pakistan, India, Thailand, Indonesia, Iran, Hong Kong on the coast of China, Japan; to Greece, Yugoslavia, Morocco, and twice to Russia. She was not the sort of visitor whose impressions of a country go no deeper than a collection of snapshots and picture postcards. She had long interviews with persons of the rank of Nehru, Marshal Tito, the King and Queen of Greece, the Sultan of Morocco, Khrushchev; but she was not content with contacts only on the high official level. Whenever and wherever she could, she got in touch with groups of ordinary people, to gain an insight into their problems, and through her concern as an American for their needs to do what she could—as she expressed it in *India and the Awakening East*—to enable other countries, and especially those of Asia, "to understand us and to believe in us and in our genuine desire to help."[30]

She came back from her world travels with clear convictions.

She recognized without evasion the tremendous material progress which had been made in Russia and in some other Communist countries, and the appeal which this would have to disadvantaged peoples in Asia and Africa who had to struggle up from nothing. At the same time she revolted from the stifling of individual freedom and the grim regimentation which Communism represented. "I think I should die if I had to live in Soviet Russia," she wrote.[31] What she wanted intensely was to see America and the other nations which have had the great heritage of freedom actually show to the disadvantaged peoples that the civilization of the West, with its Christian belief in the dignity of every man, can offer to human beings everywhere the fullness of life they crave. So when she came home she grasped every opportunity to meet with the young, to talk with college students, and to bring home as convincingly as she could even to children the truth that the privileged have a responsibility to the unprivileged, and the strong a duty to the weak; and that America can deserve and keep its greatness only if it tries to understand the problems and help to meet the needs of the rest of the peoples of the earth.

In October 1959, Mrs. Roosevelt reached her seventy-fifth birthday. "It was a busy day," she afterward wrote, "as most of mine are, with little time for introspection." But she did find herself looking back along the way she had come, and asking herself what was the best that she had learned. "I was not a gifted person," she said with that plain honesty which was always hers as she looked at herself, "but I was always deeply interested in every manifestation of life, good or bad. I never let slip an opportunity to increase my knowledge of people and conditions. . . . I had really only three assets: I was keenly interested, I accepted every challenge and every opportunity to learn more, and I had energy and self-discipline. As a result I have never had to look for interests to fill my life. If you are interested, things come to you, . . . One thing leads to another, and as you gain in knowledge and in experience new opportunities open up before you."[32] "One can, even without any particular gifts," she wrote, "overcome obstacles that seem insurmountable if one is willing to face the fact that they must be overcome; that, in spite of timidity and fear, in spite of a lack of special talents, one can find a way to live widely and fully. . . . The fatal thing is the rejection. Life was meant to be lived. . . . One must never, for whatever reason, turn his back on life."[33]

Three more years of full activity were given to her. Then in November 1962, after a brief illness with some sort of obscure cancer condition, she died; and at her death men and women from many countries and from all ranks of life paid their tribute to this extraordinary person who had seemed to begin only as her family's ugly duckling, shy and self-distrustful, but who at the end, in repeated public-opinion polls, had been ranked among the living women of the world as the one above all others the most admired. It had been true of her, as Archibald Mac-Leish, the poet, wrote, that "things got simpler where she was. Good became good again, and nonsense nonsense, and evil evil, and a man could live again and even pity. . . . She gave our time her life. All of it. Not just the end of it, the death, but all of it —the whole, full life."[34]

And Adlai E. Stevenson said of her: "She walked in the slums and ghettos of the world, not on a tour of inspection, nor as a condescending patron, but as one who could not feel complacent while others were hungry, and who could not find contentment while others were in distress. . . . She would rather light a candle than curse the darkness, and her glow has warmed the world."[35]

Notes

I. Great Women of the Bible

1. John Keats, *Ode to a Nightingale*.
2. New York: Alfred A. Knopf, 1945; pp. 12, 14-15.
3. Lenore Coffee and William Joyce Cowen (New York: Samuel French, 1939).
4. Boston and New York: Houghton Mifflin Company, 1913; pp. 259, 260-61.
5. *Sermons on Bible Subjects* (New York: E. P. Dutton, Everyman's Library, n.d. p. 231.

II. And Others Less Beneficent

1. Shakespeare, *Macbeth*, Act I, Scene 7; Act II, Scene 2.
2. *Ibid.*, Act V, Scene 1.

III. Joan of Arc

1. T. Douglas Murray (ed.), *Jeanne D'Arc* (New York: McClure. Phillips and Co., 1902) p. 221.
2. *Ibid.*, pp. 10-11.
3. *Ibid.*, p. 25.
4. *Ibid.*, p. 226.
5. *Ibid.*, p. 226.
6. *Ibid.*, pp. 223-24.
7. *Ibid.*, p. 231.
8. New York: Doubleday, Doran & Company, 1931; p. 122.
9. *Ibid.*, pp. 122-123.
10. *Ibid.*, p. 136.
11. *Ibid.*, p. 137.
12. *Ibid.*, p. 137.
13. *Ibid.*, p. 130.
14. Murray, *op. cit.*, pp. vii-viii.
15. *Ibid.*, p. 281.
16. *Ibid.*, p. 240.
17. Sackville-West, *op. cit.*, p. 141.
18. Murray, *op. cit.*, p. 236.

19. *Ibid.*, pp. 104, 114.
20. New York; Brentano's, 1924; pp. v, 75.
21. Murray, *op. cit.*, p. 133.
22. Shaw, pp. 136-137.

IV. Susanna Wesley

1. Trans. E. B. Pusey (New York: E. P. Dutton; Everyman's Library, n.d.), pp. 85, 94, 171.
2. *Ibid.*, p. 196.
3. Nehemiah Curnock (ed.), *The Journal of the Rev. John Wesley*, III (London: Epworth Press, 1938), 34-38.
4. *The Destiny of Man* (Boston: Houghton Mifflin Company, 1884), pp. 67-69.
5. New York: The Viking Press, 1962; pp. 29-30.
6. Curnock, *op. cit.*, III, 32.
7. *Ibid.*, p. 33.
8. John Telford (ed.), *The Letters of the Rev. John Wesley*, I (London: Epworth Press, 1931), 119-20.
9. Curnock, *op. cit.*, pp. 32-34.

V. Elizabeth Fry

1. Epistle to the Reader, prefixed to Fox's *Great Mistery*, as quoted in Hastings, *Encyclopedia of Religion and Ethics*, Vol. VI (New York: Charles Scribner's Sons, 1914), article on Society of Friends.
2. Janet Whitney, *Elizabeth Fry, Quaker Heroine* (Boston: Little, Brown and Company, 1936), pp. 19-20.
3. *Ibid.*, p. 12.
4. *Ibid.*, p. 8.
5. *Ibid.*, p. 15.
6. *Ibid.*, p. 14.
7. *Ibid.*, p. 37.
8. *Ibid.*
9. *Ibid.*, pp. 41-42.
10. *Ibid.*, pp. 43-44.
11. *Ibid.*, p. 57.
12. *Ibid.*, p. 66.
13. *Ibid.*, p. 68.
14. *Ibid.*, p. 71.
15. *Ibid.*, p. 85.
16. *Ibid.*, p. 91.
17. *Ibid.*, pp. 96-97.
18. *Ibid.*, p. 111.
19. *Ibid.*, p. 187.
20. *Ibid.*, p. 183.
21. *Ibid.*, p. 194.

22. *Ibid.*, p. 193.
23. *Ibid.*, p. 184.
24. *Ibid.*, p. 207.
25. *Ibid.*, p. 220.
26. *Ibid.*
27. *Ibid.*, p. 235.
28. *Ibid.*, p. 167.
29. *Ibid.*, p. 300.
30. *Ibid.*, p. 65.

VI. Florence Nightingale

1. Cecil Woodham-Smith, *Florence Nightingale* (New York: Mc-Graw-Hill Book Company, 1951), p. 5.
2. *Ibid.*, p. 9.
3. *Ibid.*, p. 12.
4. *Ibid.*, p. 29.
5. "English History," *Encyclopaedia Britannica*, IX (11th ed.), 560a.
6. Woodham-Smith, *op. cit.*, p. 31.
7. *Ibid.*, p. 34.
8. Sir Edward Cook, *The Life of Florence Nightingale*, I (London: Macmillan and Company, 1913), 100.
9. *Ibid.*, p. 111.
10. *Ibid.*, pp. 113, 114.
11. *Ibid.*, pp. 136-137.
12. *Ibid.*, pp. 146-147.
13. Woodham-Smith, *op. cit.*, pp. 87, 88, 89.
14. *Ibid.*, p. 103.
15. *Ibid.*
16. Cook, *op. cit.*, pp. 184-85.
17. *Ibid.*, p. 235.
18. *Ibid.*, p. 237.
19. *Ibid.*, p. 200.
20. Woodham-Smith, *op. cit.*, p. 170.
21. *Ibid.*, p. 144.
22. *Ibid.*, p. 166.
23. *Ibid.*, p. 181.
24. *Ibid.*, p. 178.
25. Cook, *op. cit.*, II, 434.
26. Quoted in *Ibid.*, I, v.

VII. Jane Addams

1. Jane Addams, *Twenty Years at Hull House* (New York: The Macmillan Company, 1910).
2. *Ibid.*, p. 1.
3. *Ibid.*, pp. 5-6.

4. *Ibid.*, pp. 3-5.
5. *Ibid.*, p. 5.
6. *Ibid.*, p. 18.
7. *Ibid.*, p. 45.
8. *Ibid.*, pp. 78-79.
9. *Ibid.*, p. 15.
10. *Ibid.*, p. 71.
11. *Ibid.*, p. 68.
12. *Ibid.*, p. 79.
13. *Ibid.*, p. 85.
14. *Chicago Poems* (New York: Rinehart and Winston, Inc., 1916, 1944), p. 3.
15. "The Shame of the Cities," *McClure's Magazine.*
16. Addams, *op. cit.*, p. 94.
17. *Ibid.*, pp. 103-4.
18. Hermann Hagedorn, *Americans: A Book of Lives*, (New York: The John Day Company, 1946), p. 174.
19. Addams, *op cit.*, p. 199.
20. New York: Harper & Row, 1908; p. 148.
21. Margaret Tims, *Jane Addams of Hull House* (New York: The Macmillan Company, 1961), p. 72.
22. *Ibid.*, p. 45.
23. Addams, *op cit.*, pp. 120-21.
24. *Ibid.*, pp. 125, 118, 116-17.
25. *Ibid.*, p. 127.
26. Tims, *op. cit.*, p. 93.
27. *Ibid.*, p. 133.
28. *Ibid.*, p. 130.
29. *Ibid.*, p. 136.
30. *Ibid.*, p. 137.
31. *Ibid.*, p. 141.

VIII. Virginia Randolph and Mary McLeod Bethune

1. Lance G. E. Jones, *The Jeanes Teacher in the United States* (Chapel Hill: The University of North Carolina Press, 1937), p. 24.
2. A. C. McGiffert, *Martin Luther, The Man and His Work* (New York: The Century Co., 1912), p. 4.
3. Jones, *op. cit.*, p. 26.
4. *Ibid.*, pp. 29-30.
5. *Ibid.*, p. 33.
6. *Ibid.*
7. *Ibid.*, p. 18.
8. *Ibid.*, p. 38.
9. Catherine Owens Peare, *Mary McLeod Bethune* (New York: Vanguard Press, 1951), p. 28.
10. *Ibid.*, pp. 66-67.

11. *Ibid.*, p. 89.
12. *Ibid.*, p. 95.
13. *Ibid.*, p. 109.
14. *Ibid.*, p. 137.
15. *Ibid.*, p. 190.
16. *Ibid.*, p. 150.

IX. Edith Cavell

1. Barbara W. Tuchman, *The Guns of August* (New York: The Macmillan Company, 1962), p. 1.
2. A. A. Hoehling, *A Whisper of Eternity* (New York: Thomas Yoseloff, Inc., 1957), pp. 18-19.
3. *Ibid.*, p. 23.
4. *Ibid.*, pp. 27-28.
5. *Ibid.*, pp. 31-32.
6. Tuchman, *op. cit.*, pp. 1, 14.
7. Elizabeth Grey, *Friend within the Gates* (Boston: Houghton, Mifflin Company, 1961), p. 102.
8. Hoehling, *op. cit.*, pp. 51-52.
9. D. J. Cardinal Mercier, *Cardinal Mercier's Own Story* (New York: George H. Doran Company, 1920), p. 344.
10. Hoehling, *op. cit.*, p. 99.
11. *Ibid.*, p. 100.
12. *Ibid.*, pp. 148-49.
13. *Ibid.*, p. 150.
14. *Ibid.*, p. 142.
15. Grey, *op. cit.*, p. 104.

X. Mary-Cooke Branch Munford

1. Walter Russell Bowie, *Sunrise in the South* (Richmond: The William Byrd Press, 1942), p. 27.
2. *Ibid.*, p. 49.
3. *Ibid.*, p. 162.
4. *Ibid.*, p. 165.
5. *Ibid.*, pp. 100-1.
6. *Ibid.*, p. 91.
7. *Ibid.*, p. 98.
8. *Ibid.*, pp. 103-4.
9. *Ibid.*, p. 93.
10. *Ibid.*, pp. 104, 105.
11. *Ibid.*, p. 122.
12. *Ibid.*, pp. 131, 132-33.
13. *Ibid.*, pp. 140-41.
14. *Ibid.*, p. 158.

XI. Helen Keller and Anne Sullivan Macy

1. "Laura Dewey Bridgman," *Encyclopaedia Britannica,* IV (11th ed.), 559 a.
2. Helen Keller, *The Story of My Life* (New York: Grosset & Dunlap, 1902), pp. 303-5.
3. *Ibid.,* pp. 305-6.
4. *Ibid.,* p. 306.
5. *Ibid.,* p. 309.
6. *Ibid.,* pp. 311-12.
7. *Ibid.,* p. 315.
8. *Ibid.,* p. 316.
9. *Ibid.,* p. 321.
10. *Ibid.,* p. 96.
11. Quoted in Hermann Hagedorn, *Americans: A Book of Lives* (New York: The John Day Company, 1946), p. 280.
12. *Ibid.,* p. 283.
13. Keller, *op. cit.,* pp. 96-97, 101.
14. London: Hodder and Stoughton, 1908; pp. 7, 48, 49.
15. *Ibid.,* pp. 20, 27, 21.
16. *Ibid.,* pp. 86-87.
17. *Ibid.,* pp. 103-104.
18. New York: Doubleday & Company, 1955; p. 247.
19. Hagedorn, *op. cit.,* p. 283.

XII. Eleanor Roosevelt

1. Eleanor Roosevelt, *This Is My Story* (New York: Harper & Row, 1937), p. 3.
2. *Ibid.,* p. 11.
3. *Ibid.,* p. 16.
4. *Ibid.,* p. 84.
5. *Ibid.,* pp. 100-1.
6. *Ibid.,* p. 115.
7. *Ibid.,* p. 139.
8. *Ibid.,* p. 173.
9. *Ibid.*
10. *Ibid.,* pp. 140, 202-3.
11. Alfred Steinberg, *Mrs. R., The Life of Eleanor Roosevelt* (New York: G. P. Putnam's Sons, 1958), p. 127.
12. *Ibid.,* p. 129.
13. *Ibid.,* p. 129.
14. "Compensation," *Essays,* First Series (Cambridge: Houghton Mifflin Company, 1887), p. 121.
15. Steinberg, *op. cit.,* pp. 135, 136.
16. *Ibid.,* p. 194.
17. New York: The Viking Press, 1946; p. 75.

18. Eleanor Roosevelt, *This I Remember* (New York: Harper & Row, 1949), p. 56.

19. *The Autobiography of Eleanor Roosevelt* (New York: Harper & Row, 1961), pp. 177-78.

20. *Ibid.*, p. 192.

21. *Ibid.*, p. 193.

22. *Ibid.*, p. 208.

23. *Ibid.*, p. 209.

24. *Ibid.*, p. 219.

25. *Ibid.*, pp. 283-84.

26. *Ibid.*, p. 287.

27. *Ibid.*

28. *Ibid.*, p. 299.

29. *Ibid.*, p. 308.

30. *India and the Awakening East* (New York: Harper & Row, 1953), p. 229.

31. *Autobiography of Eleanor Roosevelt*, p. 369.

32. *Ibid.*, pp. 410-11.

33. *Ibid.*, p. xix.

34. *Nation*, Nov. 17, 1962.

35. *New York Times*, Nov. 18, 1962.

Set in Linotype Janson
Composed, printed and bound by The Haddon Craftsmen, Inc.
HARPER & ROW, PUBLISHERS, INCORPORATED

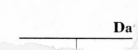